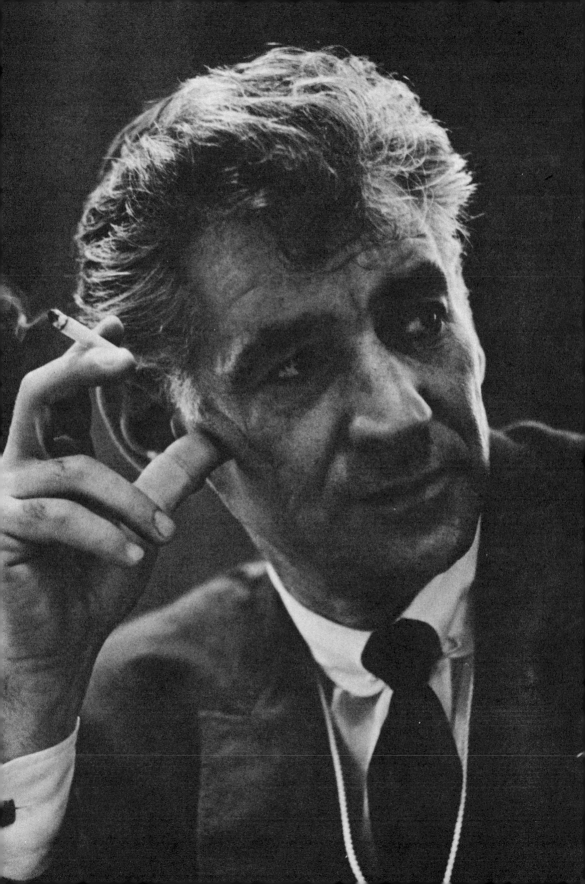

LEONARD BERNSTEIN

The Infinite Variety of Music

SIMON AND SCHUSTER ———————————

NEW YORK

LIBRARY OF CONGRESS CATALOG CARD NUMBER: 66–24038

DESIGNED BY EVE METZ

MANUFACTURED IN THE UNITED STATES OF AMERICA

The author wishes to express his gratitude for permission to reprint material from the following sources:

Ayer, Nat, *Gee! But I Like Music With My Meals:* Copyright 1911 by Jerome H. Remick & Company. Copyright renewed and assigned to Remick Music Corporation. Used by permission.

Copland, Aaron, *Appalachian Spring:* Copyright © 1945 by Aaron Copland. Reprinted by permission of Aaron Copland, copyright owner, and Boosey & Hawkes, Inc., sole licensee.

Copland, Aaron, *El Salon Mexico:* Copyright © 1939 by Aaron Copland. Reprinted by permission of Aaron Copland, copyright owner, and Boosey & Hawkes, Inc., sole licensee.

Copland, Aaron, *Third Symphony:* Copyright © 1947 by Aaron Copland. Reprinted by permission of Aaron Copland, copyright owner, and Boosey & Hawkes, Inc., sole licensee.

Gershwin, George, *An American in Paris:* Copyright 1929 by New World Music Corporation. Copyright renewed. Used by permission.

Gershwin, George, *Rhapsody in Blue:* Copyright 1924 by New World Music Corporation. Copyright renewed. Used by permission.

Joplin, Scott, *Maple Leaf Rag:* Permission granted by Larrabee Publications.

Milhaud, Darius, *The Creation of the World:* Published with the authorization of Editions Max Eschig, Paris, world copyright holders.

Porter, Cole, *Begin the Beguine:* Copyright 1935 by Harms, Inc. Copyright renewed. Used by permission.

Prokofieff, Serge, *Symphony No. 5, Op. 100:* Copyright © 1956, 1958 by MCA Music, a division of MCA, Inc., New York. Used by permission of Leeds Music Company, New York. All rights reserved.

Ravel, Maurice, *Bolero:* Permission for reprint granted by Durand & Cie, Paris. Copyright owners, Elkan-Vogel Co., Inc., Philadelphia, Pa., sole agents.

Ravel, Maurice, *Daphnis et Chloe:* Permission for reprint granted by Durand & Cie, Paris. Copyright owners, Elkan-Vogel Co., Inc., Philadelphia, Pa., sole agents.

Satie, Erik, *Parade* : With the permission of Editions Salabert S.A. France, 22 rue Chauchat, Paris. Copyright 1917 by Rouart Lerolle.

Schoenberg, Arnold, *Opus 33A:* Copyright 1929 by Universal Edition Vienna. Copyright renewed 1956. Used by permission of Universal Edition.

Shostakovich, Dmitri, *Symphony No. 5, Op. 47:* Copyright © 1945 by MCA Music, a division of MCA, Inc., New York. Used by permission of Leeds Music Company, New York. All rights reserved.

Strauss, Richard, *Der Rosenkavalier:* Copyright © 1910, 1911, 1912 by Adolph Furstner; renewed 1938. Copyright and renewal assigned to Boosey & Hawkes, Inc. Reprinted by permission of Boosey & Hawkes, Inc.

Strauss, Richard, *Salome:* Copyright © 1905 by Adolph Furstner; renewed 1933. Copyright and renewal assigned to Boosey & Hawkes, Inc. Reprinted by permission of Boosey & Hawkes, Inc.

Stravinsky, Igor, *Firebird:* Reprinted by permission of the copyright holder, J. & W. Chester, Ltd., London W. 1.

Stravinsky, Igor, *Ragtime for 11 Instruments:* By permission of the copyright holder, J. & W. Chester, Ltd., London, W. 1.

Stravinsky, Igor, *Rite of Spring:* Copyright 1921 by Edition Russe de Musique. Assigned to Boosey & Hawkes, Inc., 1947. Used by permission of Boosey & Hawkes, Inc.

Styne, Jule, *The Party's Over:* Copyright © 1956 by Betty Comden, Adolph Green, and Jule Styne. Chappell & Co., Inc., sole and exclusive selling agent.

"A Sabbatical Report" first appeared in *The New York Times,* under the title "What I Thought and What I Did," on October 24, 1965.

"The Muzak Muse" first appeared in *Show* magazine, under the title "Nobody Listens Anymore, George," in February 1962.

FOR FELICIA, WITH LOVE

A GRATEFUL ACKNOWLEDGMENT IS DUE TO HENRY SIMON, WHO FOR THE THIRD TIME HAS GODFATHERED A BOOK OF MINE; AND TO THE MESSRS. GOTTLIEB, ROBERT AND JACK, UNRELATED TO EACH OTHER EXCEPT BY THE KINSHIP OF ZEAL AND CARE WITH WHICH THEY EDITED THESE COMPLEX PAGES.

LB

CONTENTS

INTRODUCTION

An Open Letter

MY DEAR AND GENTLE READER:

Everyone says that this is a critical moment in the history of music. I agree, but double in spades: it is a *scary* moment. The famous gulf between composer and audience is not only wider than ever: it has become an ocean. What is more, it has frozen over; and it shows no immediate signs of either narrowing or thawing.

It has been claimed that the abovementioned gulf first appeared as a tiny fissure the moment a composer first set down his personal message, conceived in his own unconscious rather than in the collective unconscious of the sacred/secular community. This may well be; and, if true, makes our gulf hundreds of years old. But throughout this period—even in the wildest years of Romanticism—there has always been some relation between composer and public, a symbiotic interaction that has fed both. The composer has been the manipulator of musical dynamics, responsible for change and growth, creating the public taste and then satisfying it with the appropriate nutriment; while the public, *quid pro quo*, has nourished him by simply being interested. Any new opera, by Monteverdi, Rossini, Wagner or Puccini has in its time invariably been an occasion for curiosity, speculation and excitement. Likewise a new symphony of Haydn or Brahms, a new sonata of Scarlatti or Chopin.

This is no longer true, nor has it been true in our century. The First World War seemed to mark a full stop: Debussy, Mahler, Strauss, and the early Stravinsky barely made the finish line; they were the last names in that long era of mutually dependent composer and public. From then on it became a hassle: composer *versus* public. For fifty years now audiences have been primarily interested in music of the past; even now they (you) are just catching up with Vivaldi, Bellini, Buxtehude, Ives. The controversy backs and fills about Wagner, as though he were Stockhausen. We (you) are still discovering Haydn symphonies, Handel operas. And it still requires a monumental effort of concentration for the average concert-goer to absorb the *Eroica* as a full, continuous formal experience.

9

To say nothing of *Elektra, Pelleas,* or Mahler's *Seventh.* Gentle Reader, be frank and admit it.

What this means is that for fifty years the public has not anticipated with delight the première of a single symphonic or operatic work. If this seems too strong a statement, then fight back; remind me of the glaring exceptions: *Porgy and Bess* (can show tunes make an opera?); Shostakovitch's *Seventh Symphony* (a wartime enthusiasm inflated to hysteria by the competition of broadcasting networks); *Mahagonny* (a local quasi-political phenomenon). . . . The list could go on; but these works were all exceptions, and their delights anticipated chiefly for nonmusical reasons. The hideous fact remains that composer and public are an ocean apart and have been for half a century. Can you think of any other fifty-year period since the Renaissance when such a situation obtained? I can't. And if this is true, it signifies a dramatic qualitative change in our musical society: namely, that for the first time we are living a musical life that is *not based on the composition of our time.* This is purely a twentieth-century phenomenon; it has never been true before.

We could conceivably look at this drastic change with equanimity, form a quasi-scientific opinion about its causes, and even project an objective theory as to its probable future course—if it were not for the fact that we are simultaneously living with such an incredible boom in musical activity. Statistics are soaring: more people are listening to more music than ever before. And it is the intersection of these two phenomena—the public's enormous new interest in music, plus their total lack of interest in *new* music, the musical bang plus the musical whimper—that has created this scary moment.

I am a fanatic music lover. I can't live one day without hearing music, playing it, studying it, or thinking about it. And all this is quite apart from my professional role as musician; I am a fan, a committed member of the musical public. And in this role (which I presume is not too different from yours, gentle Reader), in this role of simple music lover, I confess, freely though unhappily, that at this moment, as of this writing, God forgive me, I have far more pleasure in following the musical adventures of Simon & Garfunkel or of The Association singing "Along Comes Mary" than I have in most of what is being written now by the whole community of "avant-garde" composers. This may not be true a year from now, or even by the time these words appear in print; but right now, on the 21st of June, 1966, that is how I feel. Pop music seems to be the only area where there is to be found unabashed vitality, the fun of invention, the feeling of fresh air. Everything else suddenly seems old-fashioned: electronic music, serialism, chance music—they have already acquired the musty odor of academicism. Even jazz seems to have ground to a painful halt. And tonal music lies in abeyance, dormant.

These depressing reflections are hardly ones calculated to catapult my readers into the body of this book, hungry for musical joys. If I were my editor, I would chuck out this introduction and replace it with one short inspirational paragraph. But I am not my editor; and I can only hope that he will understand that these thoughts are precisely the background against which this book is conceived. No, I will not look around me at the busy but barren musical scenery and pack myself off into hibernation until the buds appear. I will stay right here and loudly proclaim the infinite variety of music.

And right here, dear Reader (if you are still with me and have your wits about you), you will pull me up short. How can you contend (you will ask, I hope) that there is infinite variety, hence untold aspects of beauty, still to be revealed, if this change is qualitative? How do you reconcile the gulf with the hope? I have two answers. The first is simple, reverse logic: If I believed in the permanence of that gulf I would have to disbelieve in the validity of musical communication, of our psychic speech; and I would then no longer wish to live in this world. But I do want to continue living in this world, and therefore musical communication (warmth, understanding, revelation) must be valid. I wish there were a better word for *communication;* I mean by it the tenderness we feel when we recognize and share with another human being a deep, unnameable, elusive emotional shape or shade. That is really what a composer is saying in his music: *has this ever happened to you? Haven't you experienced this same tone, insight, shock, anxiety, release?* And when you react to ("like") a piece of music, you are simply replying to the composer, *yes.*

My second answer is simpler still, although it may take a little longer to say it. The gulf is temporary; the change, though qualitative, is transitional. The critical moment through which we are living, extended though it may be into an era, cannot define music in terms of its future. It is a moment of waiting, of flux.

Having said that I believe this musical crisis to be transitory in nature, I must now say where the transition may be leading, and why. I think that the key is to be found in the nature of music itself. It is an art so distinct, so utterly different from all other arts, that we must be careful not to assign to it values and dynamics it does not have. This is the mistake so many people make who follow the arts as a whole and try to deduce generalizations about them. What works in other arts does not necessarily work in music. Let us, for the sake of argument, try for a generalization. What is the nature of this crisis in all the arts today? We are constantly hearing negative phrases: anti-art, anti-play, anti-novel, anti-hero, non-picture, non-poem. We hear that art has become, perforce, art-commentary; we fear that techniques have swallowed up what used to be known as content. All this is reputed to be lamentable, a poor show, a sad state. And yet look at how many works of art, conceived in something like these terms, prosper, attract a large following, and even succeed in moving us deeply. There must be something good in all this negativism.

And there is. For what these works are doing is simply moving constantly toward more poetic fields of relevance. Let us now be specific: *Waiting for Godot* is a mightily moving and compassionate non-play. *La Dolce Vita,* which deals with emptiness and tawdriness, is a curiously invigorating film, even an inspiring one. Nabokov's non-novel *Pale Fire* is a thrilling masterpiece, and its hero, Charles Kinbote, is a pure non-hero. Balanchine's most abstract and esoteric ballets are his prize smash hits. De Kooning's pictures can be wonderfully decorative, suggestive, stimulating and very expensive. This could become a very long list indeed; but there is one thing that it could not include—a piece of serious anti-music. Music cannot prosper as a non-art, because it is basically and radically an abstract art, whereas all the other arts deal basically with real images—words, shapes, stories, the human body. And when a great artist takes a real image and abstracts it, or joins it to another real image that seems irrelevant, or combines them in an illogical way, he is poeticizing. In this sense Joyce is more poetical than Zola, Balanchine more than Petipa, Nabokov more than Tolstoy, Fellini more than Griffith. But John Cage is *not* more poetical than Mahler, nor is Boulez more so than Debussy.

Why must music be excluded from this very prosperous tendency in the arts? Because it is abstract to start with; it deals *directly* with the emotions, through a transparent medium of tones which are unrelated to any representational aspects of living. The only "reality" these tones can have is *form*—that is, the precise way in which these tones interconnect. And by form I mean the shape of a two-note motive as well as of a phrase, or of the whole second act of *Tristan.* One cannot "abstract" musical tones; on the contrary they have to be *given* their reality through form: up-and-down, long-and-short, loud-and-soft.

And so to the inescapable conclusion. All forms that we have ever known—plain chant, motet, fugue, or sonata—have always been conceived in *tonality,* that is, in the sense of a tonal magnetic center, with subsidiary tonal relationships. This sense, I believe, is built into the human organism; we cannot hear two isolated tones, even devoid of any context, without immediately imputing a tonal meaning to them. We may differ from one another in the tonal meaning we infer, but we infer it nonetheless. We are stuck with this, and always will be. And the moment a composer tries to "abstract" musical tones by denying them their tonal implications, he has left the world of communication. In fact, it is all but impossible to do (although Heaven knows how hard composers have been trying for fifty years)—as witness the increasingly desperate means being resorted to—chance-music, electronic sounds, noteless "instructions," the manipulation of noise, whatnot.

It has occasionally occurred to me that music could conceivably exist, some distant day, ultimately detached from tonality. I can't hear such music in my head, but I am willing to grant the possibility. Only that distant day would have to have seen a fundamental change in our physical laws, possibly through man's detaching himself from this planet. Perhaps he has already begun, in his space-chase, the long road to that New Consciousness, that Omega point. Perhaps we are some day to be freed from the tyranny of time, the dictatorship of the harmonic series. Perhaps. But meanwhile we are still earth-based, earth-bound, far from any Omega point, caught up in such old-fashioned things as human relationships, ideological, international, and interracial strife. We are not by any stretch of the imagination planet-free, the wish dreams of our cosmologists notwithstanding. How can we speak of reaching the Omega point when we are still playing such backyard games as Vietnam?

No, we are still earth creatures, still needful of human warmth and the need to communicate among ourselves. For which the Lord be praised. And as long as there is reaching out of one of us to another, there will be the healing comfort of tonal response. It can be no mere coincidence that after half a century of radical experiment the best and best-loved works in atonal or 12-tone or serial idioms are those works which seem to have preserved, against all odds, some backdrop of tonality—those works which are richest in tonal implications. I think offhand of Schoenberg's Third Quartet, his Violin Concerto, his two Chamber Symphonies; almost all of Berg's music; Stravinsky in *Agon* or *Threni;* even Webern in his Symphony or in his second Cantata—in all of these works there are continuous and assertive specters of tonality that haunt you as you listen. And the more you listen, the more you are haunted. And in the haunting you feel the agony of longing for tonality, the violent wrench away from it, and the blind need to recapture it.

We will recapture it. That is the meaning of our transition, our crisis. But we will come back to it in a new relationship, renewed by the catharsis of our agony. I cannot resist drawing a parallel between the much-proclaimed Death of Tonality and the equally trumpeted Death of God. Curious, isn't it, that Nietzsche issued that particular proclamation in 1883, the same year that Wagner died, supposedly taking tonality to the grave with him? Dear Reader, I humbly submit to you the proposition that neither death is true; all that has died is our own outworn conceptions. The crisis in faith through which we are living is not unlike the musical crisis; we will, if we are lucky, come out of them both with new and freer concepts, more personal perhaps—or even less personal: who is to say?—but in any case with a new idea of God, a new idea of tonality. And music will survive.

Sincerely,
LEONARD BERNSTEIN

FAIRFIELD, CONNECTICUT
June 21, 1966

I

An Imaginary Conversation

THE MUZAK MUSE

The scene is a luxurious jet plane, soon to be obsolete, hissing westward after the sun as if to overtake it and prevent the advent of night. The seat next to mine is vacant, and I have installed in it, as I often do on long journeys (and have since childhood), the disembodied person of George Washington, my faithful traveling companion, to whom I have long been in the habit of explaining the wonders of jets, automobiles, electric lights, billboards, drive-ins, and all the other wonders that have cropped up in the hundred and sixty years since he last laid eyes on this land. It is an exciting game, because he is always so excited and wide-eyed at each new miracle. He also serves a fine purpose, which is that of an ideal interviewer, a provoker of thoughts. In this capacity he is flawless, for he always asks the right question (as if he knew precisely what I wanted to say), and never makes extended speeches of his own.

G.W. is basking in the hushed wonder of Muzak, which is brainwashing the plane; I am trying hard to escape from it into any reading matter at hand.

G.W.

(*Dreamily*): Mmm. Miracle of miracles. A truly heavenly miracle, music of the spheres . . .

(*I continue to read. He gets the point. Another tack*):

G.W.
What are you reading?

L.B.
Funny you should ask that now. Here on page one of the London
Times Literary Supplement there is something that should fascinate
you, and fill you with pride. "In its darkness and its light the American imagination has become the most powerful stream of Western
thought and culture. It was born out of the European Reformation;
and it was sustained by Europe until it broke free into independent
life. Now we in Old Europe see in New Europe a vast vigour . . ."
Doesn't that make you proud? Could you have foretold in 1789 that
a British newspaper would one day be saying such things about their
erstwhile colonies?

G.W.
(*Contentedly*): I always knew it would be so. Of course we had to
come to this. Leaders of Western culture. Jets. Muzak.

L.B.
You can skip the Muzak. But as usual you've provided me with my
next thought. Fanatic that I am, I naturally translate everything I
read and hear into musical terms, and I was thinking as I read that
extraordinary paragraph: is it true of us musically? Do we lead
Western musical culture? No, we don't, General Washington.

G.W.
But my dear young friend, you yourself were telling me on our last
trip about the great musical boom in this country. I believe you even
supplied statistics: concerts, summer festivals, phonograph records
by the millions—why, all America seems to be music-mad!

L.B.
Statistics be damned. All your music-mad Americans, all your orchestras and hi-fi's and stereos and festivals put together don't make

a ripple in that "powerful stream" the *Times* is talking about. What is a "powerful stream of Western thought and culture" anyway? It is the result of creativity, the result of our Faulkners and Hemingways and De Koonings and Pollocks and Hellmans and Frosts. And what do we find in the musical department? Our concert literature is still mainly European. (So are our soloists, conductors, and singers.) And all the new experiments seem to come out of France and Germany, just as it was before—Stockhausen, Webern, Boulez. Our Coplands and Schumans and Carters and Sessionses haven't had a whit as much influence abroad as the Schoenbergs and Stockhausens have had on us. Of course our jazz *has* had a big influence, but where does that put us, as leaders of Western musical culture?

G.W.
(*His patriotism wounded*): Well, as we used to say at Valley Forge, we'll *make* it happen. It's only right that we should lead in music as in everything else. (*Vigorously*): All right, what do we do about it?

L.B.
I don't know, I don't know.

G.W.
Come on, let's investigate a little. Perhaps if we discover what's holding us back, or what's in our way, we can rectify it and move on to constructive steps.

L.B.
That sounds like good Valley Forge reasoning, too. OK: for one thing, we hear too much music.

G.W.
You can't mean that! You, a musician, a spreader of the gospel—

L.B.
I didn't say we *listen* too much; I said we *hear* too much. There's a big difference between listening—which is an active experience, participating in the music, riding with it up and down and in and out

of its involvements and evolvements—and just hearing, which is completely passive. That's what we've got too much of—the eternal radio and TV set, this cursed Muzak, plaguing us from coast to coast, in jets and trains and depots and restaurants and elevators and barbershops. We get music from all sides, music we *can't* listen to, only hear. It becomes a national addiction; and music therefore becomes too undifferentiated. We reach a saturation point; our concentration is diminished, our ears are too tired for real listening. That's one trouble.

G.W.

But certainly, even if it's true, that trouble doesn't account for Roger Sessions' lack of influence abroad. I don't see the connection.

L.B.

The connection is this: music is hard. It's not easy to listen to a piece and really know and feel what's going on in it all the time. It may be easy to *take*, or pleasant to hear for many people; it may evoke fanciful images in the mind, or bathe them in a sensuous glow, or stimulate, or soothe, or whatever. But none of that is *listening*. And until we have a great listening public, and not just a passively *hearing* one, we will never be a musically cultured nation.

G.W.

You mean we are *not* a musically cultured nation? But I thought—

L.B.

No, we're not, really. Not yet, anyway; although we may be well on the way. But that's all right, don't be upset! We will be. It takes doing. Do you realize how hard it is even for a professional musician to absorb a modern 12-tone work at one hearing? I know there are plenty of musicians who pretend to be able to, but they're kidding themselves. Without having had recourse to the printed score they're in trouble with all this serial technique, with its crab canons and retrograde inversions. Why, the other day I played "Happy Birthday" backward for a very avant-garde composer, and he couldn't recognize it at all. How, then, can he recognize a 12-tone

series backward? I then addressed him by his own name spelled
backward, and he simply looked bewildered. Imagine.

G.W.
I still don't see—

L.B.
Well, if it's that hard for a trained musician, just think how hard it
is for a simple citizen (even one who likes music a lot) to listen to,
say, Brahms' First Symphony, and follow it through from beginning
to end in all its manipulated complexities, all its contrapuntal
beauties and subtleties! I don't imagine there are more than a handful of nonmusicians in all America who can do that. Do you see now
what I'm getting at?

G.W.
I see; but I don't believe you. In this great land, with all its universi-
ties and cultural establishments, a mere handful—

L.B.
A mere handful. Who can really follow it *all*. People simply don't
know what they're missing. There is so much more joy and exaltation and spiritual food to be gotten out of that Brahms First than
you get by simply enjoying the tunes, the mellow sound of the
strings, the lyrical improvisations of the woodwinds, or the majestic
utterances of the brass. There is the structure, General, the structure. The harmonic flow, the architectural build—

G.W.
Well, sir, I was never much of a music-lover myself, but I always
liked a good tune. Still, I can see what you mean. That is, if we *are*
going to be the most powerful stream and all that. Let me think.
Maybe the reason is that our visual sense is so much keener than our
aural one. Say, I think I've got it! Look; our eyes are certainly
our most important sense organ. Through them we know our
world, our loved ones, nature. Through them we read, learn, communicate. So of course we cater to them; we develop that visual

sense out of all proportion to the other four. After all, our ears aren't half so important, even though we do hear one another talk with them. But it's easier to live in this world with impaired hearing than with impaired sight. And when it comes to art the same thing is true, isn't it? People all know much more about painting and literature and architecture than they do about music, don't they? And the reason is clear. It's easier to see than to hear, more immediate, more striking.

L.B.

That's the longest speech you've ever made. But it's most interesting. In this same *Times* I've been reading about the sale of a Cézanne yesterday in London for half a million dollars. Do you think anyone in his right mind would dream of paying that for the original manuscript of a Debussy score? Never. And it's not that Debussy is any less famous or important than Cézanne; it's only that Cézanne is for the eye, therefore simple, immediately perceptible; whereas the Debussy is for the ear, and therefore difficult, removed from immediate perception, because it doesn't even live until it is performed. So what's the attraction of owning his manuscript? It's a mystery to most people, something for the initiate only. And yet the actual *pleasure* derived from music may be infinitely greater than what you get from a painting. It is more physical; it is an organized time-experience, organized for you by the composer. A painting is not; the viewer must organize his own experience by directing his own perceptions to the tree in the lower right or the sunrise in the upper left. That's why I say that people are missing so much when they don't get the *totality* of a musical experience, which is all laid out for them.

G.W.

But how can you expect people to understand a score as acutely and thoroughly as they do a painting? After all, almost nobody can read music.

L.B.

Thank you. As always, you hand me my next speech on a silver charger. Almost nobody can read music. Or if they do, it's a laborious torture of counting lines and spaces while mumbling "All Cows Eat Grass" or "Every Good Boy Deserves Fun" like perfect idiots. And here we have stumbled on at least one constructive step, as you would have said at Valley Forge: *Teach people to read music.* It's not so difficult, and it's perfectly possible to include the reading of music in the basic materials of education, like learning to read French. Why not? Either we're going to be cultured or we're not.

G.W.

(*Sleepily*): But I don't understand why reading music would make so much difference. After all, there has never been a time in the history of any country when people in general could read music, has there? Maybe the Greeks. Or, I seem to recall that young Tom Jefferson—

L.B.

Possibly. But certain societies have come close to it. Any gentleman worthy of the name in the Italian or English Renaissance could (hypothetically) read music. But what percentage of the population could that have been? Or think of the "accomplished young lady" of Jane Austen's day (of course that was after your time). Those young ladies had to have a knowledge of music as one of their "accomplishments." But it was so specifically a *ladies'* accomplishment that it had no real value. So, in general, you're right: it's never been true that reading music was a common ability in any given society. But, then, there has never been a society like ours, so democratically and universally educated, so open to knowledge. This is the perfect moment to begin.

G.W.

I grant you all that, but I still don't see why the simple ability to read notes would change people's listening habits or enable them to follow a Brahms symphony with more insight. Why is it so important?

L.B.

It's terribly important; first of all, because it is the key to the personal experience, the first-hand, active musical experience. Nothing can do so much for musical understanding as sitting down and playing music yourself. I could talk myself hoarse about Mozart on a thousand television shows and never convey to you a fraction of the insight and knowledge you could gain from an hour of playing Mozart sonatas all by yourself. And no book on Beethoven symphonies can tell you as much as you can absorb by playing four-hand versions of them with your favorite partner. Someday I must tell you about John Dewey, who advocated learning by doing. It's a great idea, especially for music; because by actually *playing* music over and over we absorb all those dusty abstract rules of form and harmonic structure and the rest almost by osmosis, by feeling and sensing their rightness. It is learning without tears; the facts of music are no longer dry facts, but living truths. And once these truths are instilled in the great musical public, they will automatically be equipped to *listen* actively, to participate in each musical work they are offered. Don't you see?

(*Pause. G.W. is mulling it over.*)

L.B.

(*Pursuing the advantage*): And what's more, there would then begin to exist a body of terminology common to all, which would make *real* discussion of music possible, not just social nattering about how the conductor took the second movement too fast, or about rival prima donnas.

(*Pause. There is a faint clicking of dental plates.*)

L.B.

(*Climactically*): But there's an even more important result in the offing—music in the home. Think how important that is—not just listening to the phonograph but making music in the family! That is perhaps the chief essential for a "cultured" musical community. Think of that new day for chamber music, for chamber singing. Think of the life force music would receive from this new demand for sonatas and duets and trios and quartets and madrigals and glees and motets! Then we would indeed have a solidly grounded, personally oriented musical life; and out of it would most certainly arise a vast new American musical literature, works that would be played and known and understood and loved. Which would make the composer a part of the living tissue of music. After all, he's the main thing, isn't he? The composer would become the fountainhead of it all—which he should be—and not some remote, embittered archangel. And then we would have our musical Faulkners and Frosts; then we would send out our influence abroad; then we would truly be that "powerful stream" the London *Times* is talking about.

(There is a long pause. Suddenly it is clear that G.W. is asleep, a happy smile on his face. The heavenly Muzak purrs on, over and around his delighted ears.)

(FEBRUARY 1962)

II

Five Television Scripts

THE INFINITE
VARIETY OF MUSIC

TELECAST: FEBRUARY 22, 1959

*The program opens with the first nineteen bars of Suite No. 2 from
Ravel's* Daphnis et Chloé.

. . . and so on for seventeen more bars.

Leonard Bernstein:
That's a lot of notes—16,206 of them in only 75 seconds of music.
And yet, among all those notes there are only 12 *different* ones.
Imagine: 12 little notes, out of which composers have been making
thousands of different pieces for hundreds of years! And no two
pieces are exactly alike, even in periods when composers were
writing very much like one another, as in Palestrina's time, or in the
period between Bach and Mozart, or, for that matter, right now,
when even computers manage not to duplicate one another. Each
piece, however unoriginal or unimportant, manages to be literally
different from every other piece.

Now, just think what a situation a novelist would be in if he had
only 12 words in his language: *if, and, but, bread, circus, taxes,
love, hate, forgive, hop, skip* and *toothbrush.* Try and make *War
and Peace* or *Moby Dick* out of those. In fact, try to make one
sensible statement. Yet lo, the poor composer, who has nothing but
12 notes to work with. Of course, we're talking about Western music
specifically, and not about Hindu music, for example, which uses

scales that may contain 22 different notes. But even so, it seems like a miracle. How can it be that those Occidental oceans of different musical works come out of just one dozen notes? We're going to try and answer that question and see if we can get some inkling of the creative process that causes this magic to happen.

(L.B. goes to the piano)

Let's start with some facts and figures. We already know that we have 12 notes to work with, the notes of what is called the chromatic scale. Let's say we start with A:

Piano:

A   a♯   b   c   c♯   d   d♯   e   f   f♯   g   g♯   A

—which has brought us to another A, at which point the 12-note scale starts all over again. Now there are 88 keys on the piano, from this:

to this:

—all of which are those same dozen notes repeated over and over again in different registers. In terms of the orchestra, there is a deep, deep bass register:

Contrabassoon:

then the normal bass register:

Trombone:

then a tenor register:

Bass clarinet:

a mezzo-soprano register:

Viola:

a soprano register:

Oboe:

and finally two octaves more of super-soprano register:

Flute, then Piccolo:

until we arrive at those famous sounds that only dogs can hear.

So all in all, coming back to the piano, we have more than we bargained for: we have the 12-note scale seven and one-third times; that is to say, the same scale in over seven different registers. That's already a big enlargement of scope, but of course it's an enlargement on the most primitive level—by simple *repetition* of scales, higher or lower. But the whole point of musical creation, however, is not to write those notes in scale-wise order only, but to *change* their order so as to produce melodic meaning.

Let's take those 12 tones, in any one register, and see what the possibilities are of their melodic combinations. Through an awe-striking mathematical formula,* it turns out that the maximum number of

---

* I am grateful to Stefan Mengelberg for providing the following mathematical data:

The number of melodic fragments from one to twelve notes, not permitting repetition of any note within a fragment and disregarding octave displacement, rhythmic variation, timbre, etc., is given by:

$$\sum_{i=1}^{12} \frac{12!}{(12-i)!} = 1{,}302{,}061{,}344.$$

Of this number, 479,000,600 are complete twelve-tone rows, in which every chromatic note occurs once. By "verticalizing" these sequences we obtain the same number of "chords" of one to twelve tones without doubling. The order of tones from fundamental up is taken into account, but not the spacing.

To consider combinations of melody and harmony, we compute the number of arrangements up to twelve melody notes in length, none repeated, with the harmony changing no more frequently than the melody note. Harmonizations may be up to twelve notes thick, subject to the restrictions above. We have:

$$\sum_{n=1}^{12} \frac{K^n \cdot 12!}{12^n \cdot (12-n)!} \quad \text{where } K = 1{,}302{,}061{,}344.$$

To introduce the possibilities of *register*, we take the 88 pitches of the piano keyboard as our basic materials instead of the twelve chromatic notes. We then have as the total number of melodic fragments up to 88 notes in length (no note repeated in its own octave, and other restrictions as above):

$$\sum_{i=1}^{88} \frac{88!}{(88-i)!} \simeq 50{,}419 \text{ followed by 130 zeros.}$$

The number of possible chord combinations is given by $2^{88} - 1 \simeq 309\frac{1}{2}$ septillion. Sequences of n such chords can be constructed in $(2^{88} - 1)^n$ different ways. For $n = 12$, this yields approximately 77,214 followed by 313 zeros. (Chord repetition is allowed here.)

As soon as note repetition is permitted in melodies, the number of possibilities becomes infinite, $\aleph$ (aleph-null), and when rhythmic variation is introduced, the number of possibilities becomes infinite to an even higher order.

S.M.

possible melodic combinations of these 12 notes is the following astronomical figure: one billion, three hundred and two million, sixty-one thousand, three hundred and forty-four, without ever repeating any one note in any one pattern. Incredible! But enormous as that seems, it's still a finite number; and you'd think that eventually even *that* number of combinations would be exhausted. However, musical science supplies even further possibilities, so all is not lost. Remember that our number of possibilities so far has been limited to music that consists of only one note at a time moving horizontally, as melody. Just think how it all expands wildly when the vertical idea of harmony, or chords, enters the picture. Obviously the number of possible combinations of the 12 tones *as chords* is also one billion, three hundred and two million, and so on. Now we have all the possible melodic combinations *plus* that same number of chords to go with them; and each one of those chords can conceivably go with each one of the possible melodic combinations! We begin to smell infinity.

My mathematician friends tell me that the maximum possible number of vertical *and* horizontal combinations of 12 notes or less comes to a figure which is expressed in 106 digits. The actual round figure, for those of you who are curious about such things, is 127 followed by 103 zeros. You may have heard of the word *googol*, which was invented as much for convenience as for humor, to express in shorthand any number consisting of a digit followed by 100 zeros, much the same way as astronomers use the word *light-year* to avoid having to spend their time mumbling endless numerical expressions. Well, melodically and harmonically speaking, we already have at our finger tips 127 googols of possible combinations. And on top of that, consider the element of counterpoint—different melodic lines going on at once—which means that it is also possible to combine all those billion odd *melodic* combinations with each other! At this point the brain begins to reel. It's like counting stars in the Milky Way. And we haven't even taken into account the all-important element of rhythmic variety, which provides a whole *new* Milky Way of possibilities—to say nothing of the whole range of tempo, or speed; to say nothing of innumerable instrumental colors, vocal colors, and the like—all of which add galaxy upon galaxy to this musical universe, whose limits are by this time beyond calculation.

It turns out, after all, that the realm of music is an infinity into which the composer's mind goes wandering, looking for *his* material, *his* way of selecting and shaping it. And that's the most important component of all—the individual composer, the mind and heart with *something to say*, something to communicate through this vast mathematical language. I'd like to try to show you how some composers have availed themselves of this infinite musical variety, because I think that through such an exploration we can also get a glimpse of the infinite variety of the creative human spirit.

To make the game a little easier, let's confine ourselves to a melodic pattern of 4 notes, instead of all 12—just 4 simple, very familiar notes such as these:

Piano:

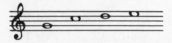

which we all know and love as:

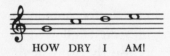

Let's see what amazingly different musical shapes they can assume, what an abundance of musical meanings those notes can have. And let's further restrict ourselves to pieces of music in which these 4 notes are the *first* 4 notes of the main melodic material.

You may know a little French folk song called "Il était un' Bergère":

What distinguishes that charming tune is its light, gay, skipping quality, the fact that it's in 6/8 time, that it goes at a certain tempo, *and* that the 4 notes we're interested in are arranged so that the first one:

is an upbeat, or a weak beat; that the second one:

is a downbeat, or a strong beat, and so on.

But now here's another melody that also begins with "How Dry I Am," the theme from Smetana's symphonic poem *The Moldau.* It's also in 6/8 time, in about the same tempo, with the 4 notes arranged exactly as in the French song, but look at how different it is: *

You see, it's not light and gay any more, but majestic and sweeping. Why is this? Just because it's louder and fuller? No, it's because of the *shape* of the melody, because of what comes *after* those first 4 notes. The little French song went up the 4 notes, and then modestly down again:

but the *Moldau* theme keeps going up:

---

* For the convenience of the reader, this example and all that follow in this script are given in the key of C.

making a broader line, a bigger arch. That's the real difference. Smetana's tune simply has a different aesthetic message from the one contained in the little French folk song. But remember, the possibilities of change are infinite.

For instance, all we have to do is to take the same 4 notes and make the first one a downbeat instead of an upbeat, then put it into 3/4 time, and we have a whole new melody:

I'm sure you know that one—Lehar's famous "Merry Widow" Waltz.

Now all we have to do is keep that first note on the downbeat, make all the notes equal, slow it up a bit, and presto change-o, here's Handel's "Water Music":

Orchestra:

Nothing to it. Ah, but there's a lot to it. Remember that these are not just tunes; they have their own harmony, their own orchestration, and—most important—their own shape. It's what happens *after* the first 4 notes that's crucial to the shape of the melody, how it moves and breathes, whether it acquires a long line or is broken into short sections. For example, here are two melodies with the same springboard of those 4 notes, equally stressed as in Handel's tune. One is by Schubert and one by Beethoven. Both melodies begin literally with our exact formula. But the Schubert melody, which is from his beautiful cello sonata called the "Arpeggione," breaks in half at its mid-point by *re*stating the 4-note formula:

Cello and piano:

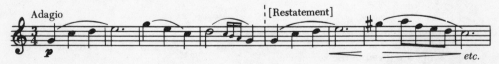

The Beethoven melody, on the other hand, which is from his Second Symphony, does not repeat its opening phrase at all, but goes on inventing anew for the whole eight bars. You get the effect, then, of a much longer line, one single, uninterrupted line, like this:

Orchestra:

You see the difference? The two melodies begin almost exactly alike, but have entirely different consequences.

Here's an example of an even longer line, a bigger arch, deriving from the same initial 4 notes. Listen to this theme from Brahms' First Piano Concerto, and watch how those notes now expand into a fuller, more romantic melody:

Piano:

But perhaps the greatest "How Dry I Am" festival of all takes place at the end of Richard Strauss' famous tone poem *Death and Transfiguration*. He builds his whole final apotheosis on a theme that begins with just those 4 notes, with the first one acting as an upbeat:

but which then leaps up an octave:

thus producing this wide-open, monumental, transfigured melody:

Orchestra:

As we play it for you, you will hear it in the strings, in the harp, in the winds, and in the brass—each time with a new *coloristic* meaning. You may also detect it toward the end being played twice as slowly by the horns:

and then twice again as slowly by the trombones:

all being devices that make new varieties. And it all ends up in a starry, mystical exaltation of How-Dry-I-Ams, climbing from the lowest register to the heights of heaven.

(*Here the orchestra performs the last six minutes of* Death and Transfiguration.)

You may now think that we've followed those 4 notes to their ultimate flowering; but we have only *begun* to investigate the different ways of handling them. The staggering truth is that there is a whole new Milky Way of possibilities. This series of 4 notes has been used by very dissimilar composers to create music of great beauty and variety. For example, let us again take them as the beginning of a melody, but this time vary them by simply repeating one or two of them before writing the others. Let's say we write down note number 1 *twice*:

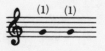

then after note number 2 go back to note 1, and then to 2 again:

then take note number 3, repeat it; and add note 4:

What we have written is nothing less than the nocturne theme from Mendelssohn's *Midsummer Night's Dream.* Isn't that amazingly simple?

French horn:

Another charming example of this kind of variation by repeating notes is the little Shaker hymn tune used by Aaron Copland in his ballet *Appalachian Spring.* It derives from the same 4 notes, of course, only with the second note repeated, and the tune comes out like this:

Clarinet:

But this device of note repetition is still only one of many ways in which our 4-note formula can be varied. For instance, we can take the 4 notes and ornament them with very simple dissonances, thus getting a whole new shape and meaning. Now a dissonance in this sense does not mean anything particularly unpleasant; it means only any note that doesn't belong strictly to the harmony of the moment. For instance, take a popular song called "The Party's Over," from the Broadway musical *Bells Are Ringing*. The composer, Jule Styne, has written a phrase that is basically "How Dry I Am," only he's added a dissonance called an *appogiatura,* a technical word that means a note that leans on another note. In other words, it is a dissonance that has to resolve to another note that's *not* a dissonance. And so a song is born:

L.B. sings:

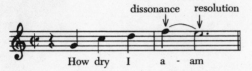

or, in the words of Comden and Green:

In much the same way Richard Strauss again uses a dissonance to vary the same formula in *Till Eulenspiegel*. Do you remember the famous horn theme?

Horn:

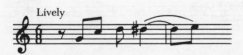

That captivating motive is nothing but our old 4 notes with a new dissonance this time ornamenting it, and then resolving to the last note:

But now we come to one of the most important ways of varying our formula—through what is called permutations, that is, simply changing the *order* of the 4 notes. For example, I'm sure you all know the sound of the Westminster chimes as they sound the third quarter. Those beloved phrases are *all* permutations of "How Dry I Am." The 4 notes are simply anagrammed to form each different phrase:

Piano:

So we see that Big Ben strikes three different permutations of our 4 notes, conspicuously omitting the original pattern. Another permutation those bells *don't* use is this one:

which, of course, we all know as "Sweet Adeline." Prokofieff, however, *does* use it in the final movement of his Fifth Symphony:

Orchestra:

In fact, looking back through symphonic music, we are amazed to see how often the great composers have permuted our 4 little notes. If you ever go to hear any of Wagner's *Ring* operas, you'll hear all kinds of versions of the formula. The theme of the bird in *Siegfried,* for example, is a quick, darting little fragment in which the 4 notes are used in the order 1-2-4-3:

Clarinet:

Even Siegfried's lusty horn-call is a permutation of the same 4 notes in the order 2-1-4-3:

only with note number 1 raised an octave higher, and with note number 2 repeated before note number 3 is heard. Then it's all put into vigorous hunting rhythm, and it comes out like this:

Horn:

Or, turning again to Brahms, we find one of his greatest and noblest inventions to be nothing but another simple permutation of the formula—as heard in the Westminster chimes at a quarter to every hour:

Only here, in the marvelous introduction to the finale of his First Symphony, Brahms has given these notes an extremely arresting rhythm and developed the phrase in so remarkable a way that the whole passage emerges as a kind of celestial summons:

Orchestra:

Wonderful what can happen to a simple chime, isn't it?

Even more astounding is the discovery that this same permutation turns out to be the triumphant love theme at the end of Strauss' opera *Salomé:*

Strauss really seems to be the big man in this discussion, but it is fascinating to see in how many different ways he has been able to employ these 4 notes and make them constantly different. Perhaps the greatest results he ever achieved with them occurs toward the end of his glorious opera *Der Rosenkavalier,* when the three principal voices—all female—combine in the unforgettable, heartbreaking trio. And that whole trio, mind you, is constructed out of yet another simple permutation of our formula, in the order of 3-4-2-1:

It doesn't seem too promising at first; in fact, it is first heard in the opera as a gay little drunken waltz:

Piano:

But when this tune recurs in the form of the trio it becomes one of the great moments of all operatic history.

(*At this point three singers, playing the parts of the Marschallin, Sophie and Octavian, sing the trio with the orchestra*):

Hab' mirs ge - lobt, ihn lieb zu ha - ben etc.

Well, that's a lot of permutations. But we've only scratched the surface. Those googols of possibilities are so limitless that there's always a new angle, some new way of handling them so that they seem fresh as a daisy. We haven't the space to go into all of the ways, but just as dessert, here's one more—simply putting the formula into the minor mode. You see, all the versions we've examined so far, including the straight version:

Piano:

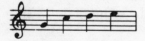

the ornamented versions, such as:

the permuted versions, such as:

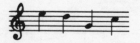

—all these versions have been in the major, because—well, because "How Dry I Am" simply *is* in the major. But all you have to do is change the last note slightly, putting it into the minor:

and a whole new can of beans has been opened up. The examples of this slightly varied formula are legion. You all know the finale of Beethoven's "Pathétique" Sonata?

Then here it is again, in a rhythmic variant, popping up as the famous tune from the *Raymond* Overture, which you may remember from silent movie days:

Orchestra:

You'd think that by this twentieth century of ours no man on earth could bear to hear those 4 notes again, to say nothing of any composer bearing to write them again. But Shostakovich could bear it and has used those same notes with spectacular results in the last movement of his Fifth Symphony. Here he builds a whole movement on it, brash and rousing. He just blurts out:

in the minor, with no permutations, no ornaments or anything. That's it, that's his tune.

And, of course, when he reaches the dazzling conclusion of the movement, there's nothing left to do but simply put it back into the major, in the brass, unashamed, no holds barred:

—at which point some of us may feel that we've *had* that tune for all time. But we must also feel the miracle that there was still *this* new flowering of "How Dry I Am" left to be written in 1937—after all those years of Handel, Beethoven, Brahms, Wagner, and Strauss —a miracle because of the inexhaustible fertility of the human mind, the infinitude of man's creative spirit.

Remember that Shostakovich was writing this work at a time of severe governmental criticism. He was trying to reinstate himself in the Soviet good graces, to conform and to please. And yet, even in conforming, by using such comfortable, familiar notes as those 4, his tremendous creative spirit was able to overcome their banality and make them into a new artistic utterance. So we might think of those historic 4 notes as a motto of man's infinite variety, his indomitable will to create afresh and to assert himself as an individual.

Tack that above your desk; it's a more effective motto than SMILE or THINK. It says REJOICE!

(*To end the telecast the entire finale of Shostakovich's Fifth Symphony was performed.*)

JAZZ IN SERIOUS MUSIC

TELECAST: JANUARY 25, 1959

Leonard Bernstein:

If this were a program called "Name That Noise," or something, and you had to identify the following musical excerpt, you might have a bit of trouble. But even if you've never heard it before, there are two things you *can* probably tell about it: first, that it's serious concert music, symphonic in its point of view, in the intricate way it develops, in its large-scale orchestral concept; and second, that it's probably American, because of certain elements in it that remind us of jazz.

Orchestra:

49

This excerpt is from Aaron Copland's Third Symphony, which is *very* symphonic and *very* jazzy. Now, offhand you would wonder how two such strange bedfellows got together. Concert music always carries with it the connotation of sobriety, spiritual uplift, deadly seriousness; while jazz connotes relaxation, improvisation, shirt sleeves—in short, fun. Maybe the difference can be expressed by saying that it's all right to talk during jazz, or laugh, or dance, or leave the room for a minute, but with symphonic music—not a word, don't move, head in hands, eyes closed in wondrous dreaming—or maybe in just plain snoozing.

But they *can* go together, these two strangers, and often do. We are going to look at two prime examples of this mating and try to discover how such an odd marriage came to be.

At the turn of this twentieth century of ours the great European tradition of symphonic music had reached a point of exhaustion. It had been building and building for over a century from Mozart to Beethoven to Brahms to Wagner, each one adding something to the size of the orchestra, to the length of the music, to the weight of the emotional statements, until by 1900 there was Mahler overpowering them all.

How much bigger could music get? It had to stop somewhere or bust. The only remedy seemed to be to throw it all overboard and start a new development, find fresh material, new devices—atonality, quarter-tone music, whole-tone scales, old Greek scales, anything, only not the Mozart-to-Mendelssohn-to-Mahler triple play that the Germans had going for more than a hundred years.

One of the strongest attractions for the composers of this new antisymphonic generation was the lure of the exotic, the far-away—the Far East, the Near East, Africa, anywhere as long as it wasn't Germany. And perhaps the most exotic attraction of all these was this very peculiar sound:

Honky-tonk piano:

Ragtime, they called it then, a half-breed music, bred in New Orleans out of African drumming and French military marches and Polish polkas. What did it have that was so enticing—the blue notes, the syncopations, the trombone smears? No. You can't reduce it to its technical components. The thing that made it irresistible was that it had *life;* it was fresh and vital—it swung. Which was just what the doctor ordered for the jaded European musician who could no longer digest the heavy German cooking of Wagner, Reger, Pfitzner and company. *This* was spicy, light, effervescent; it was Sal Hepatica.

By 1912 ragtime was in solid. There was a steady stream of rags flowing out of Tin Pan Alley.

(L.B. shows old sheet-music covers: "Spaghetti Rag," "Black and White Rag," "Alexander's Ragtime Band," "Skeleton Rag," "Ragging the Baby to Sleep," "He's a Rag Picker," etc.)

Let's look at one of the great ones, in fact the first one to appear, "The Maple Leaf Rag":

Piano:

Now just what makes this a rag? Well, first of all, it's a march, as you can hear from the accompaniment:

But over that accompaniment there's nothing anyone ever marched to before: bright, jolly, syncopated figures that make you want to dance, not march:

Its essential color is that of the honky-tonk piano; it couldn't sound better played by the greatest orchestra on earth; it belongs to the barroom:

As to its form, it's the same as any march, with contrasting trio, or middle section:

That's all there is. There's no hint of blue notes or of any of the jazz paraphernalia that was later to become so important; just pure, naïve, high spirits.

Now, imagine how sweetly all this fell upon the ears of those new

European composers, especially the ones in Paris, who were so eagerly seeking fresh, non-Wagnerian waters. Erik Satie, Debussy, Ravel, Martinů, Milhaud, Tansman, Stravinsky—they all grabbed at this new exotic tonic, drank it up, injected it artificially into their own personal styles and vocabularies, and out came music that was closer to the Moulin Rouge than to the *Musikfreundegesellschaft*. For example, here's a ragtime from Satie's ballet, *Parade*, which is just two steps beyond the "Maple Leaf Rag." It could almost be an authentic original, but every so often there appears some complexity or unexpected turn that reveals the hand of a sophisticated European composer.

Piano:

You see what I mean? That couldn't possibly be Tin Pan Alley. But this is nothing compared to the sophisticated treatment the rag got from *some* European composers. Stravinsky turned out no fewer than three ragtimes, one more complicated than the other, none of them even vaguely comprehensible in New Orleans or in Tin Pan Alley, but still arising out of ragtime. Here's a bit from Stravinsky's "Ragtime for 11 Instruments," one of which is that most unraggy Hungarian instrument called the cimbalom. Try to imagine, as you hear it, what fun Stravinsky must have had as he wrote it, back in 1918.

Orchestra:

As you see, we are now entering the domain of what is called "serious music." Not just a fox trot here, a bunny hug there; this was meant to be first-class music, several cuts above the level of sheer entertainment. And this was still only the beginning. By now we've reached the exciting 1920's, and the word *ragtime* is a thing of the past. In its place stood the blazing new word *jazz*, which had evolved from ragtime but was far beyond it. It had many more subtleties: it showed more Negro influence, like those blue notes we did not find in ragtime, and much more variety of tone color, being essentially a music for orchestra rather than solo piano; it was more involved, more sophisticated, less "square," less ricky-ticky.

All these changes are reflected in the music of those European composers who were still avidly drinking at this exotic American well. Only now instead of a ragtime by Satie you got a Charleston by Martinů, a shimmy by Hindemith, and a fox trot by Ravel. Out of all this has come one real masterpiece, one full-length, fully developed jazz work that had such character and originality that even today it sounds as fresh as it did when it was written in 1923. It is a ballet called *The Creation of the World,* by the brilliant French composer Darius Milhaud. I take the liberty of calling this work a masterpiece because it has the one real requisite of a masterpiece—durability. Among all those experiments with jazz that Europe flirted with in this period, only *The Creation of the World* emerges complete, not as a flirtation but as a real love affair with jazz.

Who can explain this phenomenon? After all, Milhaud's experiment was just as artificial as the others, just as self-conscious in its attempt to crossbreed two kinds of music from two sides of the Atlantic. But his experiment bloomed into a beautiful flower, while the others remain experiments, fascinating but slightly freakish. The only answer is in the music itself. Let's have a look at it.

First of all, it's written for a very small orchestra—at least by the old symphonic standards—a handful of strings, a few solo woodwinds including a saxophone, two trumpets, one horn, one trombone, one piano, and naturally, lots of percussion. This conglomeration may have been partly modeled on the jazz bands Milhaud says he heard when he visited this country, though what jazz band had flutes and cellos in it I can't imagine. What I suppose it really is is a cross between an idealized jazz band and the typically French refinement of Milhaud's thinking. After all, that's the way French composers *were* thinking: "The Germans puffed music up; we're going to shrink it down."

Milhaud's score begins with, of all things, a prelude and a fugue. The prelude starts innocently enough, with a sweet, almost Bach-like melody:

Orchestra:

that has no hint of jazz in it beyond the fact that it's played on a saxophone. But as soon as the first phrase is finished, two trumpets sneak quietly in with a lick, or a break, or a fill, as the jazz boys say:

which gently makes its low-down comment. From there on, the

whole prelude spins out in alternation between those two opposing ideas, one tender and noble, the other low-down and jazzy; and by some magic of musical invention they combine to make unforgettably lovely music.

Then into this tender mood breaks, surprisingly, a jazz fugue, savage, percussive, mean, but always controlled by that refined Gallic hand:

It's an extraordinary mixture: those dirty blue notes and syncopations:

and the elegant way they are handled by this chic little French orchestra—and in a fugue, at that—a real, 14-karat, scholarly fugue in the great tradition of European counterpoint. And if you think that's scholarly, listen to this place where the fugue theme and that first Bach-like theme are played at the same time; that's as scholarly as you can get. Here are the two themes together, one in the flute and one in the cello:

But it's just that strange mixture of the barbaric and the highly civilized that controls the tone of the piece right through to the end. For example, the main motive throughout the music is that group of notes known and loved by millions as "Good Evenin' Friends":

Piano:

But this phrase in Milhaud's delicate hands assumes a new lyricism, as in this delicious passage:

Orchestra:

You see how strongly the composer's personality shines through, even through these brash, low-down materials? And even in the all-out Dixieland chorus, toward the end of the piece (*see opposite*):

—with everyone blaring out his own tune in free-for-all counter-point—there is a neatness of touch, a clarity and precision that is absolutely French, absolutely Milhaud. You are constantly aware of the hand of a master.

(*The orchestra, at this point, performs the entire work.*)

ORCHESTRA

etc.

Now that we've heard the jazz masterpiece of European music, I think it would be very illuminating, and only fair, to have a look at its opposite number in our own country. Just about the time that Milhaud was writing his *Creation of the World,* a greatly gifted young American named George Gershwin was making an immortal experiment called *The Rhapsody in Blue.* There are many who will quarrel with the word *masterpiece* in connection with this work, but it can't be denied that no other American piece has so captured the imagination of people all over the world as has the *Rhapsody,* with its unfailing melodic invention and its rhythmic and harmonic inspiration.

Gershwin was exactly in the opposite position from Milhaud, who had to *learn* jazz; Gershwin had to learn how to write symphonic music. After all, he was basically a song writer—a great one, but still a student as far as orchestration, form, and symphonic technique were concerned. Yet both composers, in their different ways, were doing the same thing: making a conscious effort to fuse jazz with long-hair music. Only Milhaud's conscious effort was to borrow the foreign jazz elements and plant them in the rich soil of his own personal symphonic style, whereas Gershwin's effort was to borrow the techniques of European symphonic tradition, in order to have a soil in which to plant his natural bursting seeds of jazz. They came from different sides of the tracks, that's all—Gershwin from Tin Pan Alley, and Milhaud from the much more sophisticated alleys behind the Eiffel Tower. Hearing Gershwin's piece is like biting into a fine, big, juicy apple and letting the juice trickle freely down your chin, while hearing Milhaud's is more like taking to the same apple with an elegant fruit knife and fork, carefully peeling it, and savoring one proper bite at a time. For Milhaud was an antiromantic, a neo-classicist, sick of big, lush sounds; whereas Gershwin was a naïve, romantic American, unashamed, expansive, wonderfully old-fashioned. Just look at how he treats that same "Good Evenin' Friends" phrase that Milhaud uses so delicately. In the *Rhapsody,* where again it's the key motive of the whole piece, it comes out like this:

Piano:

Nothing refined there. Or else he makes standard, routine sequences out of it, like this:

and again, this:

Up and up, in the tried and true technique of Liszt and Tchaikovsky. But that was practically the only way he knew of developing an
idea. For instance, when he comes to develop this beautiful tune:

again he has to resort to the same sequence treatment:

And as for the form, well, it's just one section after another loosely
strung together by cadenzas. Like this:

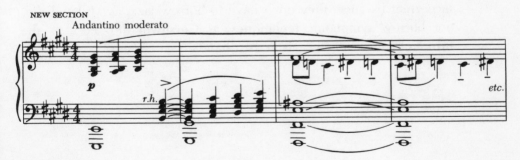

You see, *The Rhapsody in Blue* is so sectional and choppy that you can cut it, interchange the sections, leave out half of it, play it backward, play it on the piano, or organ, or banjo, or kazoo; but whatever you do, it's still *The Rhapsody in Blue.* Why? Because those *tunes* are so great. The sheer invention in it will never· grow stale.

If you're tempted to criticize Gershwin harshly or not take him seriously, remember this: the tragedy of Gershwin was his dying in his thirties, at the very moment when his techniques were finally beginning to fructify, the moment when he had finished his finest work, *Porgy and Bess.* For who knows what the next work might have been? Who knows to what heights this enormously gifted man might have raised those raw jazz materials that he had brought with him from the other side of the tracks?

(The Rhapsody in Blue *is performed here.*)

Many American composers since Gershwin have turned jazz to far subtler and more complex uses than he did. For many of them jazz entered their blood stream, became part of the air they breathed, so that it came out in their music in new, transformed ways, not sounding like jazz at all, but unmistakably American. Such composers as Copland, Harris, Schuman, and even Sessions and Piston, have written music that is American without trying, the result of an unconscious metamorphosis of jazz elements or jazz feelings. This has been one of the strongest conditioning forces of the American musical language.

But there is an even more recent generation of young American composers who are constituting a further development of this theme. They are equally at home in both worlds of jazz and the concert hall; they have both graduated from conservatories and written way-out arrangements for Stan Kenton. And their music is in perfect balance; they don't have to borrow jazz, as Milhaud did, nor borrow symphonic techniques, as Gershwin did. Perhaps the future of American music is in their hands.

THE AGELESS MOZART

(The New York Philharmonic in Venice)

TELECAST: NOVEMBER 22, 1959

(*The orchestra begins with the overture to Mozart's* Marriage of Figaro.)

Leonard Bernstein:

This performance of the overture to Mozart's opera *The Marriage of Figaro* is our most affectionate postcard to all our American friends from this glorious city of Venice. We are having a wonderful time, wish you were here, regards to all. But why Mozart? Why are we American musicians playing Austrian music in an Italian theatre? I think you'll see why instantly, if you just look around this breathtaking jewel of an opera house, known as La Fenice.

(*The camera scans the interior of the house.*)

65

An early engraving of La Fenice in Venice.

It is the embodiment of what we think of as eighteenth-century beauty. Just look at the aristocratic elegance of these proportions; the intimacy of the grandeur, which is of course the most aristocratic element of all; the lightness and airiness of the structure; the delicate gaiety of the paintings; the refined ornamentation of the scrollwork; the precise, tasteful extravagance of it all.

When we see all this, what is it that we hear? What is the first sound in our inner ears? Mozart, of course, who represents to most of us elegance, wit, daintiness, intimacy, and the rest. If this were all, however, then Mozart would have remained always an artist of his time, a rococo genius who captured his epoch in notes. But, then, so did some other composers called Stamitz and Dittersdorf capture their epoch, and so did a lot of other names you may never have heard of, including several of old Johann Sebastian Bach's sons, who left behind what had come to be regarded at the time as papa's stuffy style, with its hard-working fugues and fuddy-duddy counterpoint. These composers had embarked on this charming new garden path of late eighteenth-century prettiness—easy, refined, tuneful, witty, gay music for the "let-'em-eat-cake" nobility. But today they are mostly just admired names, while Mozart is, and always will be, the divine Mozart: not a name, but a heavenly spirit who arrived in this world, remained some thirty-odd years, and then left it new, enriched, and blessed by his visit.

What makes the difference? Only this: that Mozart's genius was a universal one, like that of all great artists. He captured not only the feel and smell and spirit of his age but also the spirit of man, man of all epochs, man in all the subtleties of his desire, struggle, and ambivalence. When we were in Moscow a month ago,* I heard the great Boris Pasternak say, "In spite of everything I am full of joy; my art exists as a record of the tragedy of human existence; it is nourished by tragedy; and my art is all my joy." So it is with our greatest creative spirits; so it was with Mozart. Which may come as something of a surprise to some of you who have the habit of equating Mozart with aristocratic delicacy and nothing more. How many people have I heard dismiss him as "tinkly," as a musical snuff-box

* On the ten-week European tour in 1959, sponsored by the President of the United States' Special Fund for Cultural Exchange. This Venice concert took place during the eighth week.

composer! Isn't this how most people were first introduced to
Mozart:

Piano:

"None of this mincing drawing-room stuff for me," such people
say. "Give me *guts* in music—Beethoven, Brahms, the tragic, the
monumental . . ." This kind of talk can mean only one thing: that
they don't *know* Mozart. No one can have listened to Mozart, listened hard, with both ears, without experiencing what Pasternak
called the "tragedy of human existence." Just listen to these few
bars from his Fantasy in C:

Tinkly, is it? Why, it could easily be Beethoven in one of his typically tragic rages. It has the power, the attack of a giant. In this
Fantasy there is even a Beethovenesque mystery, a certain veiled
wonder and awe, which is one of Mozart's most moving qualities:

Do you feel that melancholy, that tragic essence, even encased as
it is in an eighteenth-century frame? Mozart's music is constantly
escaping from its frame, because it cannot be contained within it.
No matter how clearly every bar of it is labeled 1779 or 1784, the
music is essentially timeless. It is classical music by a great romantic.
It is eternally modern music by a great classicist.

Now, in order to understand how Mozart's music escapes from its
frame, we must first understand what that "frame" is, that eighteenth-century encasement in which this music finds itself. Try to
think of this eighteenth-century period as you know it from reading
and paintings and, well, yes, even from the movies. We know it as
an era of manners, of conformism (at least among the gentry), a

time of great formality, with a huge amount of attention being paid to style, to courtly gesture, to modes of dress, to elegance of behavior, to stately forms of address, and the like. This naturally caused a vast set of patterns to arise, to which it was necessary for a cultured lady and gentleman to adhere; and this was true not only of social patterns but also of musical ones, since music always reflects its own time. That is why eighteenth-century music is so filled with patterns and formulas, amounting almost to clichés.

Take the instance of cadences. As you know, cadences are the harmonic progressions by which phrases of music are brought to a close, much as the comma, colon, and period bring word-phrases to some kind of resting point. Now if you go through the complete works of Mozart, some rainy afternoon, you will find to your horror the same cadence—patterns used with incredible repetitiveness in work after work, movement after movement, even phrase after phrase. These cadences are almost no longer music; they seem to have become only points of punctuation. For example, here is a typical Mozartean cadence, from the slow movement of his Prague Symphony.

L.B. at the piano:

Now, that is a charming cadence. But if you count up the times Mozart has employed that identical sequence of notes:

in his collected works, you would be tempted to accuse him of simply repeating himself.

No modern composer would ever permit himself such stock-in-

trade repetition. (Except bad ones, mainly of the avant-garde.) What
does it mean? That Mozart was played out? That he lacked inventiveness? Certainly not. Invention was Mozart's middle name. It
means only that he was a composer of his time, that his vocabulary
was necessarily delimited by the conventions of his time. The wonder is not that he used conventional formulas, but that, using them,
he was able to create such amazing variety. Listen to that same
cadential formula as it appears in another rhythm in his G Major
Piano Concerto:

—same notes, but different music. Then, later in the same concerto,
instead of just repeating it literally, he varies it this way:

And all through his works we can find the same cadence in different
disguises, like this, for instance:

or this:

You see? It's always the same cadence, but varied each time to
acquire a new meaning of its own, which is exactly right for the

particular passage it punctuates. And so it has ceased to be a formula
at all. That's the power of Mozart.

Now, here's another case of formula-composing. If we examine
Mozart's accompaniment figures—the supports for his melodies—we
find again a series of repeated clichés. This, for instance:

—which is known in the trade as the "Alberti bass," perhaps the
most overworked fixture of eighteenth-century music. We usually
associate it with that tinkly snuffbox we spoke of before:

But over and over again we can find Mozart using this figuration in
such a way that it is transformed by the sheer beauty of his melodic
invention above it; as, for example, in the second movement of that
same tinkly sonata, where the delicate intricacy of the melodic line
makes the Alberti accompaniment seem new and lovely:

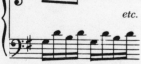

Or listen to this surprisingly romantic theme from the G Major Piano Concerto, replete with Tchaikovskian sighs and longings, and yet all riding over that same, simple-minded Alberti bass:

But even more impressive is what happens to that theme when Mozart develops it later on in the cadenza:

We have been taken clean out of the eighteenth century. The theme has now acquired a new force, an almost Beethovenesque intensity, and without yielding up for a moment that "doodle-doodle" left hand. You can see again how Mozart has transcended the limitations of the formula by the power and depth of his own invention.

So we begin to discern what this eighteenth-century frame is made of: cadence formulas, accompaniment formulas like Alberti basses, or repeated figurations like this:

or triplet figures like this:

This last figure is a case in point. I don't know if you are familiar with the great C Major Piano Concerto, whose second movement begins with just those triplets. But when an unbelievable melodic line begins to soar above it, the mechanical little accompaniment becomes in itself a thing of rare beauty, especially orchestrated as it is with delicious pizzicato basses and subtle woodwind reinforcement. I find it one of the special treasures of all musical history:

What an extraordinary experience that melody is—timeless, ageless; and yet it rests on a rigid, formal eighteenth-century pedestal.

But perhaps the most characteristic element of all in this period of stylization is the whole business of eighteenth-century ornamentation, the trills and turns and shakes and roulades that adorn the melodies of this period, just as a scrollwork "doo-dad" adorns a cornice in this Fenice Theatre. It amounts almost to a compulsion. The eighteenth-century composer, committed as he was to prettiness and aristocratic frippery, couldn't just write a tune and leave it alone. He had to decorate it with elegant icing. Just imagine how *untypical* that famous tinkly tune we heard before would sound without its ornamental mordent or turn:

Not the same thing at all, is it? But with the ornament placed on that next-to-last note, it suddenly becomes an old eighteenth-century friend:

ornament

Now, Mozart, that angelic voice, could take even that "doo-dad" and make great emotional music with it. Here is a theme from one of his violin sonatas (K.379), passionate, strong, full of pulsing drive. And yet it is actually built out of that same frilly ornament:

Violin:

Can you imagine how that music would sound without the decorative frill? Like this:

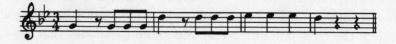

All wrong. Bare and ordinary. It's the ornament that makes the excitement:

So it turns out that Mozart has actually used the ornament itself for deep musical values and not only for eighteenth-century icing.
    But these ornaments aren't limited only to turns, or to trills:

or to grace notes:

They even run to whole scale passages and complex filigree. For instance, in a highly ornate cadenza, Mozart may write what is basically this note pattern:

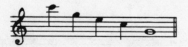

but he adorns it in this dashing way:

What a difference that makes! Not only because of that brilliant descending scale but also because it plunges the end of the phrase into a register two octaves lower, giving it a much more meaningful and moving quality.

Such are some of the ways in which Mozart constantly moves above and beyond his period, bursting out of his formulistic frame, and even using those very formulas in his own way to produce music of surprising originality and power. It is a power that enabled him to produce works of towering strength, far indeed from the musical snuffbox in which people so often lock him up. Take one of his minuets, for instance; what could be more antipowerful than a dainty minuet? And yet there stands that muscular minuet from his G Minor Symphony, utterly transformed through the strength and ingenuity of its rhythms into a movement of rich pathos and grandeur:

Orchestra:

Some dainty minuet! Why, the rhythmic variety and surprises in those few bars could be typical of a twentieth-century composer, so bold and new do they sound. And, as for power, only think of the "Jupiter" Symphony, in particular the strength of that contrapuntal last movement, which looks back to Bach for its massive fugal complexity, its virility and architectural thrust:

Orchestra:

Tremendous power! Or think of the dramatic power generated by the *operatic* Mozart, who could project human character through music to an uncanny degree—like this sudden outburst of Donna Anna's in *Don Giovanni,* which looks ahead across a whole century to Verdi:

Soprano and piano:

Why, that could almost be right out of *Aïda,* so strong is its dramatic impetus. Or listen to this passage, later on in *Don Giovanni,* the chilling moment when the ghostly statue of the Commendatore appears at supper. This is music of such depth and power that it is almost Wagnerian:

Basso and piano:

If you examine this passage closely, you find a shrinking-away from
tonality that is almost twentieth-century in quality. Some critics
have even called it "the first twelve-tone music ever written." What
strange music to come out of an eighteenth-century snuffbox! But
remember, this is not Dittersdorf; this is Mozart. And Mozart's music
transcends his period. It looks back to Bach and forward to Beethoven, to Chopin and Schubert and Verdi and even to Wagner.

Mozart is *all* music; there is nothing you can ask from music that
he cannot supply. I wish we could perform for you enough of
Mozart's music to give you the range of his emotional palette—such
works as the C Minor Mass, the Requiem, *Cosi Fan Tutte,* the E
Flat Symphony, the G Minor Quintet, and so on. But this being
obviously impossible, we are going to play for you part of one of his
great piano concertos, and I think you will find all these qualities
we have been speaking of concentrated in this one work. We are
going to play two movements, the second and third, from his marvelous Piano Concerto in G Major. If I absolutely *had* to name my
all-time favorite piece of music I think I would vote for the Andante
we are to hear now. It is Mozart at the peak of his lyrical powers,
combining serenity, melancholy, and tragic intensity in one great
lyric improvisation. You will hear the tranquillity of a Schubert *Lied,*
the filigree of a Chopin, the brooding of a Mahler. And I would
like you to be aware, particularly, of the beauty of its orchestration.
This concerto is orchestrally rather modest, even within the already
limited frame of the eighteenth-century orchestra. For instance, it
employs neither trumpets nor drums nor clarinets; and yet, wait till
you hear the wonders Mozart produces with three solo woodwinds,
blending like three glorious voices in an operatic trio, or the rich
pathos he can create with a little inner melody played by the violas.
Again, even in his orchestration Mozart has transcended his time.

(*The second movement, with L.B. conducting and playing, is heard.*)

And now we emerge from the contemplation and mystery of that
almost sacred Andante, into the brilliant light of the Finale. Brilliant
—that is the word for this marvelous rococo set of variations. The
whole movement is bathed in a glitter that could have come only

from the eighteenth century, from that age of light, lightness, and enlightenment. It is a perfect product of the age of reason—witty, objective, graceful, delicious. And yet, over it all hovers the greater spirit that is Mozart's—the spirit of compassion, of universal love, even of suffering—a spirit that knows no age, that belongs to all the ages.

(The last movement followed, concluding the telecast.)

RHYTHM

TELECAST: MARCH 13, 1960

(An actual heart is seen beating on the screen. We hear its beat):

(The image dissolves into the orchestra playing from Beethoven's Seventh Symphony):

Leonard Bernstein:
Beat, beat, beat—the fundamental pulse of all life, whether it be our blood or our breath, a pile driver, a galloping horse, or a leaky faucet. Pulse is everywhere in our lives.

83

(A split screen shows L.B. on one side, and a bass drummer's foot on the other, tapping out even, equal beats.)

At its most primitive level, it's in this drummer's foot there that is hammering away an endless series of undifferentiated beats. But how does so elemental a thing as pulse become so sophisticated an art as musical rhythm? So far this drummer is doing nothing of musical value, only 1, 1, 1, 1, 1 . . . But watch as he begins to stress any one of those beats at regular intervals.

(Drummer stresses first beat of each bar.)

BASS DRUM ... etc.

Now he is doing something. He is marking the beats off into regular groups—*1*,2,3,4, *1*,2,3,4—and pulse has suddenly become meter.

(The image of the drummer fades out, but his sound continues.)

In other words, the drummer has taken his first step toward rhythmic art by measuring and controlling sheer pulse and putting it into bars, or measures, with the strong accented beat as the first beat of each bar. But it's only the first step. Meter is only the groundwork of rhythm.

(Drummer's foot is seen.)

All right, take it a step further now as the drummer adds a rhythmic pattern over the meter.

(The camera pulls back to see the drummer's hand):

And now let's go a *hundred* steps further, as he improvises whatever rhythmic patterns he may feel necessary in order to express himself.

(Pull back to drummer, full figure. He performs a jazzy pattern):

Now we're listening to jazz—to music.

What's exciting about good jazz is on a far higher level than mere pulse or the primitive boom-boom we call meter. It's all the rhythmical intricacies, those syncopations and twists and surprises that go on *over* and *against* the beat, that make jazz swing. And this is true of all music as well, including even so meter-ridden a piece as Ravel's *Boléro,* which depends for its hypnotic effect not just on the elementary fact of its rhythmic repetitiveness but on the far more sophisticated fact that the melody, in all its languor and slinkiness, contrasts so sharply with the repetitive drumbeat:

What really attracts us is the combination of the drum accompaniment, which functions as meter, with the melodic line in its free rhythmic flow:

The parallel with poetry is immediately obvious. Certainly Shake-speare's rhythmic glories do not arise from the fact that he wrote in iambic pentameter, with five pulsations per line. If his meter alone were his rhythm, his great lines would be reduced to sheer doggerel, to say nothing of nonsense:

Oh what/a rogue/and peas/ant slave/am I!/

Is it/not mon/strous that/this play/er here . .

But you get the point. The meaning is *"Oh,* what a *rogue,"* not "Oh, *what* a *rogue";* which necessitates an inversion of that first iambic foot into a trochaic foot.

Oh what/a rogue

So Shakespeare has already built rhythmic variety into his meter, transforming it from a stupidly regular singsong into a meaningful phrase with a free rhythmic flow contained in the meter, just as the free-flowing *Boléro* melody is contained in *its* meter.

Furthermore, no actor can possibly deliver the syllable *rogue* in the same space of time as the syllable *peas–,* for instance. *Rogue* demands time, it is a big, majestic syllable; but *peas–* is a quick, light syllable, to be followed instantly by *–ant,* making *peasant.* So it is all too obvious that this line cannot be read with regular stresses, that is, in strict meter. The duration of the pulses must vary with the meaning and the rhythmic beauties of Shakespeare's invention.

(*L.B. declaims*):

"OH what a ROGUE and peasant SLAVE am I!"

There *is,* of course, poetry that demands strict delivery, precisely for the effect of monotony:

BOOTS—BOOTS—BOOTS—BOOTS—
MOVin' UP and DOWN aGAIN!

Or for the effect of primitiveness:

THEN I SAW the CONgo,
CREEPing THROUGH the BLACK,
CUTting THROUGH the JUNgle
WITH a GOLden TRACK.
BOOMlay, BOOMlay, BOOMlay, BOOM.

Or for the effect of childishness:

> I have a little shadow that goes in and out with me,
> And what can be the use of him is more than I can see.

But in these examples there is no real question of rhythm, except in its most elementary form, which is meter.

Now meter by itself is a pretty dull subject. The mere knowledge that those verses I just quoted are in trimeter or tetrameter or whatever is not exactly fascinating information. It's the same with musical metrics—2/4 time, 6/8 time, or "12/90" time. Technicalities. But as soon as we move on to the larger aspects of rhythm the subject does become fascinating. It's not so much that drummer's foot we want to know about:

Bass drum:

—it's what he's doing upstairs, with his hands:

Tenor and bass drums:

Now, even if you don't recognize that rhythmic pattern of the great funeral march from Beethoven's "Eroica" Symphony:

Piano:

you do recognize how solemn, measured, and even expressive of grief are those halting little figurations:

You see, the rhythmic pattern alone—even without the melodic notes, or the harmony, or orchestral color—just the *rhythmic design* can be expressive in itself. Over that same old 4/4 meter:

Bass drum:

there can be infinite varieties of rhythmic patterns, like this:

Wood block and bass drum:

That's the last movement of Mendelssohn's "Italian" Symphony—gay, skipping, vital:

Piano:

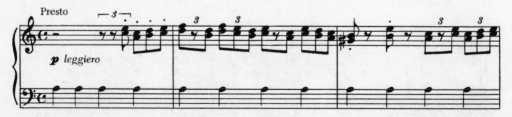

As kids we used to have a guessing game something like this, tapping out rhythms of famous tunes. See if you can tell what this one is, with the same meter going on underneath:

Snare and bass drums:

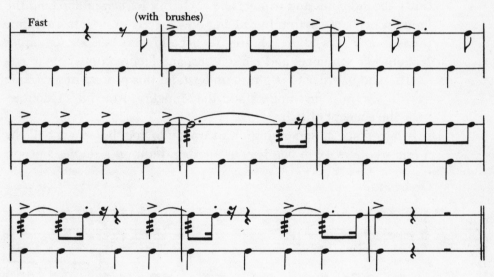

You don't have to know that tune from Gershwin's *An American in Paris* to feel its jazzy, bouncy quality:

Piano:

Those rhythmic patterns are jazzy all by themselves; in other words, rhythm is capable of conveying expressivity, even emotional content.

Now, again, it would be mere technicality to try to analyze these rhythmic patterns, to fill you with facts about dotted notes and thirty-second notes and triplets and such. But we *can* understand the larger aspects of rhythm by tracing how meters grow into rhythmic phrases, and how those phrases then build into periods, or larger sections like sentences and paragraphs, and finally into whole movements. And in order to begin to understand this process of rhythmic growth we must first understand the almighty principle of doubleness, the concept of *two*.

It may come as something of a surprise to you, but almost all the music we know is, in one way or another, built on a duple concept.

Orchestra:

Thus Mozart. *And* Beethoven:

and Brahms:

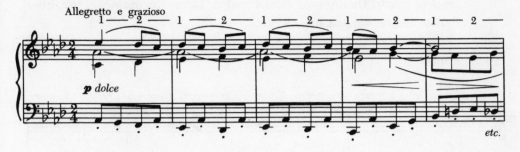

and Cole Porter:

and everyone else.

Why do we seem to need this duplexity so badly? The answer is simple. Just think again of the human heart. Its pulse is not just 1, 1, 1, 1. In order to contract and pump its supply of blood into our arteries, the heart must first expand. Thus there are *two* phases to each heartbeat, expansion and contraction, 1-2, 1-2. *That* is the fundamental beat of all life. Physical life is duple. We live in a world of up and down, back and forth, day and night. In order to exhale we must first inhale; there is no third step in the process, no intermediate function. It is in and out, in and out, 1-2, 1-2.

This is the symmetry our bodies are based on. We are creatures of the left and right, and in our center beats our heart, dutifully pumping its systole and diastole, 1-2, 1-2, as long as we live.

And so, two-legged creatures that we are, we walk left-right, left-right into the art of music. That's why most music has duple meter, which means two beats per bar or some multiple of two beats per bar, like four, six, or eight. But musical duplexity is by no means limited to anything so simple as two beats in a bar; in fact our biological need for duplexity is so great that even the *bars* themselves tend to group themselves dualistically. Take, for example, the Beethoven theme we just mentioned:

Piano:

It *has* two beats per bar, all right, but if we play the first bar alone:

we have only an abortive group of notes. This bar obviously needs to be married to a complementary second bar to achieve even the most elementary musical sense:

All right, we have two bars so far, but they are still fairly abortive. In order to arrive at a single phrase—not even a sentence, just a phrase—we need another pair of bars to balance the two we already have. So here they are:

Now we have a four-bar phrase, or two times two, but it is still incomplete musically:

So how do we complete the musical sense and make the phrase into a whole sentence? Simply by supplying another matching four bars, to lend symmetry to the four we already have:

Finally we have a full statement, in eight bars, which is two times two times two:

But Beethoven still has more to say before he is satisfied that he has written a complete melody; and of course what he does

is to marry his eight-bar theme to yet another eight bars that will
balance it and round it out:

So there is the full theme, now sixteen bars long—or two times two
times two times two. As you see, it's a simple geometric progression
and it's all duple, from the basic metrical unit right up through the
completed melody. In fact, the whole history of music can be viewed
as a development of dualistic thinking.

At this point I'm sure many of you are itching to call my attention
to my flagrant disregard of that other most important rhythmic concept, that of *three*. After all, isn't there just as much music in triple
time as there is in duple? What about waltzes, mazurkas, boleros?
What about the "Eroica," Mozart minuets, Beethoven scherzos?

What about Schubert's Unfinished Symphony?

And thousands more like it?

All right, let's have a look at tripleness. Of course it's true that much music is triple. One might even say that the three-concept is almost as fundamental as the two-concept. But note that I say *almost;* because three, basic as it is in music, is *not* grounded in our biological nature. It is not *physical* in its function. The heart just doesn't beat in 3/4 time, Viennese propaganda to the contrary. Try to imagine how life would be if we were triply constituted instead of duply. Imagine having three steps in breathing: inhale, then laterally to another lung, then out. Railroad tracks that go triangularly instead of back and forth. The compass with three points instead of four, and people with three eyes to see them with. The mind reels. We *are* duple; perhaps that's part of our finiteness. If we could break through it we might begin to understand the universal problems that plague us. But the value of tripleness, to music at least, lies precisely in the contrast with dupleness. It is the first and noblest exception to our natural savage instinct of left-right. Three is an *invented* number; an intellectual number, it is primarily an *unphysical* concept. Perhaps that is why 3 has always been so mystical a symbol to man, as in the Holy Trinity.

Now we have reached the critical point in our understanding of rhythm. Having investigated what pulse is and how it becomes meter of a duple or a triple kind, we are now in possession of the key to all the rhythms that lie beyond us, however many they are, or however complex they may get. For all rhythmic considerations from here on result in one way or another from the interaction of physical 2 and intellectual 3: either 2 *plus* 3, or 2 *times* 3, or 2 *against* 3, or whatever. Just as in arithmetic all numbers, except 1, can be reduced to the basic elements 2 and 3: four is 2 plus 2; five is 2 plus 3; six is 2 times 3; seven is 2 plus 2 plus 3; and so on to infinity.

In the same way all music is reducible to some combination of twoness and threeness. For example, let's take the most familiar triple meter we know, the waltz:

Piano:

1-2-3, 1-2-3, over and over. That's the basic unit of the waltz. But it's a rare waltz indeed that doesn't group these threefold units into twofold patterns. For instance, here's a bar of a Strauss waltz:

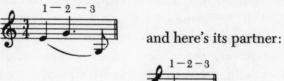

and here's its partner:

Either one alone is meaningless, but together, as the saying goes, they make beautiful music:

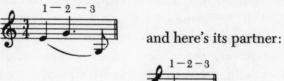

You see? 2 times 3. Again, duplexity. And the waltz is even subject to the same duple multiplications that we saw in the theme from Beethoven's Ninth Symphony. The first pair of bars is complemented by a second pair:

Then that whole four-bar group is again complemented by another:

And so on until the end of the piece. Why should this be? Why should a waltz, whose greatest claim to fame is that it's in three-quarter time, turn out to be just as much a slave to dupleness as anything else? Simply because a waltz is a dance, and a dance is performed on two legs. It's not 1-2-3, 1-2-3, 1-2-3, ad infinitum, but it's *left*-2-3, *right*-2-3, *left*-2-3, *right*-2-3. You see, it's left-right after all. The *meter* may be triple, but in the larger rhythmic sense a waltz is every bit as duple as a march.

In fact, in the great body of Western music as we know it up to our own century, triple units almost always come under the tyranny of our biological duple compulsion. Look at Wagner's popular "Ride of the Valkyries." There's a piece that at first glance seems to have broken out of its duple prison, since each bar has nine beats in it, which is 3 times 3. No hint of 2. In other words, the triple unit of the waltz is not duplicated, as in Strauss, but triplicated:

Orchestra:

But even here, once we have accepted that combination of thrice-three as our basic unit, we find as surely and clearly as in the Strauss waltz that Wagner goes on to balance each nine-beat bar with another nine-beat bar, thus immediately restoring biological order and symmetry. Once having said:

he must now answer with:

And on he goes, balancing those 2 bars with another 2 in absolute symmetry:

And then those four bars are balanced again by four others, and so on, and so on, according to the good old formula of dual multiples.

In all the music we have heard so far, whether duple or triple, there is one great factor in common: symmetry, that precise balance that derives from the physical biformity of the human being. This biformity creates in us a biological need, which then becomes an aesthetic demand. That's why so much of the music we know and love is composed of beats that combine duply and symmetrically into bars, and bars that combine symmetrically into larger formal sections, which finally comprise a complete symmetrical movement. There is something so comfortable, so stable in this anthropomorphic procedure that it has become the very spine of Western music up to our own century. Our century, of course, is quite another matter; and we'll see about that a little later.

But right now let's consider a beautiful piece of super-duple symmetry out of the nineteenth century, the finale of César Franck's

Symphony in D Minor. This is an exciting movement, but it is also
a highly stabilized one, comfortable almost to the degree of well-fed
self-sufficiency. And the root of all this comfort and satisfaction is
in its over-all symmetricality. Whatever happens once must happen
immediately a second time; whatever happens on the left must be
matched by a similar happening on the right. Just take the world-
famous second theme from this movement. A two-bar phrase, and,
of course, in duple meter:

Orchestra:

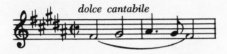

Now come the balancing two bars with a slight melodic variation:

Now four bars to balance the four we've already got:

And then all eight bars over again, in a higher key:

Utter symmetry, composure, well-being—that same stability one feels
in late Victorian painting and architecture, which is perhaps a reflection of the economic security and general sense of confidence
that is so typical of this period. Anyway it's a provocative thought,
which you might keep in the back of your mind whenever you listen
to this great hymn to symmetry, the Finale of the Franck symphony.

*(The orchestra plays the complete movement to end Part One of the
program. Part Two opens with the orchestra playing)*:

What has happened? Something wild has been going on in our century—a rhythmic revolution, led by the formidable Stravinsky, who in this great monument to rhythm, *The Rite of Spring,* unleashed forces that have all but annihilated the comfortable symmetries of yesteryear. How had Stravinsky arrived at rhythms of such jaggedness and irregularity in the few decades that separated him from César Franck? Let's see if we can track it down. It's perfectly true that unequal meters and unequal rhythmic patterns are also to be found in the great music of the past. The only difference is that such instances of asymmetry in the eighteenth and nineteenth centuries are notable precisely because they are exceptional. They represent moments of inspired freshness, or madness, if you will, in the minds of composers for whom symmetry was always the normal state of affairs; whereas in our time asymmetry has almost become the norm.

For example, Brahms was never one to reject a good five-bar phrase when it occurred to him, and five is certainly not a symmetrical number. Here the basic metrical ingredients of 2 and 3 are juxtaposed to make five, which is a new wrinkle of a sort. Do you know that lovely theme in the third movement of his First Symphony, which begins right away with a five-bar phrase?

Orchestra:

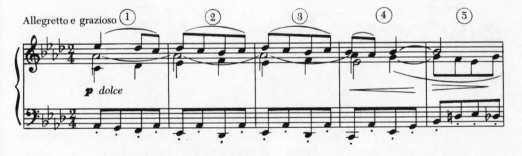

Very unusual, and very pretty indeed. But notice that even this melody becomes symmetrical in the end, since Brahms atones for his daring use of a five-bar phrase by immediately supplying a second complementary five-bar phrase, in the very same rhythmic pattern, thus restoring our good old dualistic balance:

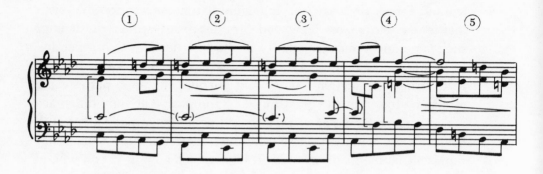

So after all Brahms couldn't get away from the biological necessity of left-right; he had to keep his symmetrical soul unruffled.

Again, we can find Tchaikovsky experimenting with asymmetry in his Sixth Symphony. Do you remember the famous second movement, a sort of three-legged waltz in five-quarter time?

Orchestra:

This is a *really* new wrinkle: five beats per bar. 12345, 12345. Or, if you wish, 12,123—12,123; again that asymmetrical juxtaposition of 2 and 3. But Tchaikovsky is also stuck in his century. This music is still bound by the old duple conventions, which require that each bar of five, irregular though it may be within itself, must be symmetrically balanced by another identical bar of five. And this convention holds true right to the end of the movement, in strict accordance with the time-honored formula of pairs of pairs of pairs. Besides, and more important, the structure within the five-beat bar never varies: it is always 2 plus 3, never 3 plus 2.

As we come closer to our own time—for example, in Stravinsky's *Firebird*—we go a step further toward asymmetry: we find a seven-beat bar, constructed as 3 plus 2 plus 2:

Orchestra:

and complemented by another seven-beat bar, but of a *different* construction, namely 2 plus 2 plus 3:

Now we're approaching modern music. At this point we are faced with metrical combinations of 2 and 3 that would have staggered the imagination of Brahms or Tchaikovsky, but which are still simple as pie compared to what is to come. After all, these two Stravinsky bars do form a balanced, though unsymmetrical, pair; and what's more, as a *pair* of bars they are further balanced by an exact reduplication, just like old-fashioned music. This is the way the two *pairs* of bars sound together:

Do you feel the symmetry? We are still in its grip, although we've certainly come a long way from César Franck. We now have meters of sevens and fives, all kinds of combinations of 2 and 3, but they still maintain some kind of regularity. Once a stretch of music starts in seven it stays in seven and remains in some sort of duple balance. But the next step finally shatters this whole convention, as modern music begins to appear in which the meter actually changes from bar to bar, from six beats in a bar $(3 + 3)$ to five $(2 + 3)$ to seven $(2 + 2 + 3)$, and so on. Like this passage from Aaron Copland's exciting work *El Salón México:*

Piano:

That's twentieth-century rhythm. There's a great new excitement in this music because of constant rhythmic surprise. You never know what's coming next. You can't tap your foot to it, regularly, secure and comfortable in the knowledge that the next bar will arrive on time, just where expected, or that it will all multiply nicely into balanced duplexities. Oh, no. Just try to tap your foot to this passage from the same Copland piece:

You can break your ankle trying to keep time to that one. But that's exactly what makes it so exciting; it has a brand-new kind of

rhythmic vitality. But where is all this leading us? Has modern
music simply gone crazy and abandoned good old regular meter forever? No, but I think we *have* come to depend in the past far too
much on symmetry, even sometimes mistaking symmetrical balance
for beauty. Why should we remain forever slaves of our two-legged-
ness? Beauty does not mean symmetry; it *does* mean balance, but
balance is not necessarily symmetrical. (And this is as true of the
music of Bach and Mozart and Beethoven as it is of Copland.) Copland's *El Salón México* is as striking an example of rhythmic uses
in our time as you can find, produced by an American composer
who has been nurtured on jazz as well as on Stravinsky and Brahms.
It is also a perfect example for our purposes because it is so compre-
hensive. Far from being constructed entirely in irregular meters and
rhythmic patterns, it ranges over the whole rhythmic universe, from
the simplest to the most complex elements, beginning with a plain
duple rhythm:

and a plain triple rhythm, sort of waltzy:

and going through all kinds of combinations of duple and triple, such as 2 against 3 simultaneously:

or 2 alternating with 3:

or 3's and 2's combined into regular patterns:

which, as you see, is a pure rhumba; and finally he goes into combinations of 2's and 3's in *irregular* patterns, which is when this piece really becomes uniquely of our time:

That's modern music, modern rhythm. We've come a long way from that simple pulsing heartbeat we started out with. Pulse has become meter, and meter has become rhythm in all its thrilling permutations. And this *El Salón México* is more than just a catalogue of the permutations; it is a masterpiece of rhythmic ingenuity and a delightful piece of Americana.

(The orchestra ended the program with a performance of the Copland work.)

Postscript: Of course rhythmic innovation now goes far beyond even the complexities of Copland and Stravinsky. In the last decade or two a curious phenomenon has become observable in avant-garde music—the multiplication of rhythmical complications to the point of creating the effect of *rhythmlessness.* After all, if many different rhythmic patterns are sounded simultaneously, or in close proximity, they tend to cancel one another out (especially with the abandonment of pulse) and create the "static" quality which is typical of much contemporary music. It is at this point that we must take leave of rhythm as we have known it on this program, much as contemporary music has taken leave of tonality.

L.B., 1966

ROMANTICISM IN MUSIC

TELECAST: JANUARY 22, 1961

(The program opens with Leonard Bernstein playing the following music on the piano):

L.B. speaking over the music:

Romantic music. Any one of you knows without the slightest clue that this is romantic music. We don't need silver candelabra on the piano to hint at it; you don't even have to know what this piece is, or who wrote it. Yet you know it was written by a composer of the romantic period. Why do you know this? Because it's warm, melodic writing? So is Mozart. Because it suggests amorous yearnings? So does Debussy. Because it's moody? So is Bach. Because it's atmospheric? So is Palestrina. Passionate? So is Schoenberg. Because it evokes images for you of palm trees gently swaying in the moonlit night, or any of a hundred other similar clichés? So does Cole Porter.

(*The piano playing stops.*)

No; this Chopin nocturne I've been playing is a romantic piece of music for specific musical reasons.

I suppose you might say that all music has something romantic about it, in the sense that all art, especially music, is a romantic aspect of human life; but that's only easy generalizing. Not one of those composers' names I mentioned can be classified as a capital-R Romanticist. Palestrina, for example, is a Renaissance composer:

Choral group:

OFFERTORY: LAETAMINI IN DOMINO

Bach is a baroque composer:

Harpsichord:

INVENTION VIII

Mozart is a classical composer:

Clavichord:

SONATA (K.331)

Debussy is an impressionist composer:

Harp:

AFTERNOON OF A FAUN

Schoenberg is an expressionist:

Piano:

KLAVIERSTÜCK, Op. 33a

But Chopin was a Romanticist. That nocturne of his I was playing has its roots deep in the hot soil of capital-R Romanticism, which was a definable historical movement, conscious and willed and organized, that took Europe like a fever in the first half of the nineteenth century. What was this fever? It was freedom-fever, a great epidemic set off by the recent French and American revolutions, nurtured by a Napoleonic age, a nationalistic upsurge, an industrial revolution, and the emergence of the middle classes. And above it all flew the banner: Freedom of the *Individual*. Under this banner the nineteenth century opened up to the ringing of such voices as Goethe, Schiller, Beethoven, and then Byron, Keats, Shelley, Pushkin, Victor Hugo, Lamartine—all shouting for freedom, for the glorification of the individual spirit, freedom from formality and stylization.

In what seemed like a moment, almost with the turn of the century, everything had changed. No longer this:

But instead, a free, heaven-bound leap, proclaiming the divine nature of free man.

No more need painters show us human beings as pretty eighteenth-
century dolls aristocratically idealized by Fragonard, but instead,

highly realistic, sometimes even ugly, perceptions—like this sketch
by Goya:

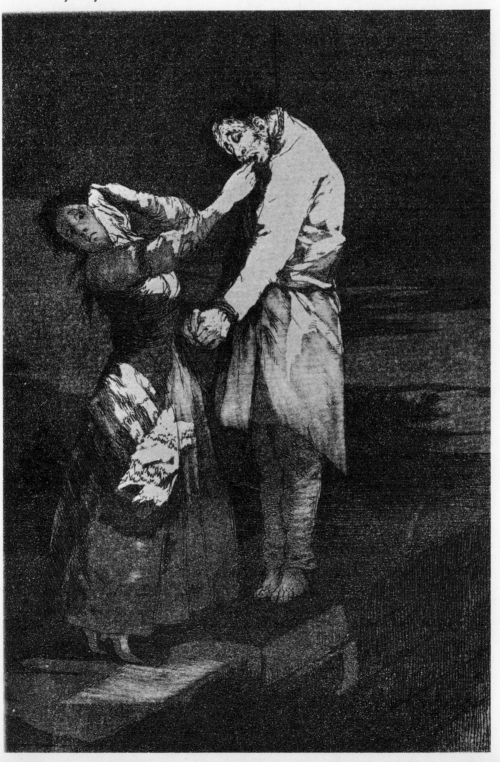

revealing not only the individuality of the subject but the personal, subjective image within the artist himself, *his* vision of a drunkard or a glutton or a male floozy. The emphasis is now on the creator, not on the object. It is how I, the artist, see life; how I, the poet, feel about the death of my friend; *I*, Edgar Allan Poe, uninhibited, unashamed of my grief.

(An actor recites):

> Ah, dream too bright to last!
>   Ah, starry Hope! that didst arise
> But to be overcast!
>   A voice from out of the Future cries,
> "On! on!"—but o'er the Past
>   (Dim gulf!) my spirit hovering lies
> Mute, motionless, aghast!
>
> For, alas! alas! with me
>   The light of Life is o'er!
>   No more—no more—no more—

L.B.:

Just contrast that romantic breast-beating with Milton mourning the death of his friend, with oh, such classical restraint:

(Another actor recites):

> Bitter constraint, and sad occasion dear,
> Compels me to disturb your season due:
> For Lycidas is dead, dead ere his prime
> Young Lycidas, and hath not left his peer.

L.B.:

All that formality goes now. The romantic says: "It is *my* self-expression that counts, not the expressions imposed upon me, whether by the royal court or the church or the stratification of classes or the tyranny of common practice. The world is changing, and I, the artist, change with it." For instance, back in the late seventeenth century, when Purcell's heroine Dido is in the throes of death, she dies to a strict *passacaglia,* one of the most classical of musical forms—sedate, courtly, and utterly objective:

Alto, with orchestra, sings "Dido's Lament":

It is very beautiful and moving music, but it is not *romantic* music. Just compare with it Wagner's heroine, Isolde, dying two hundred years later in a transcendental delirium, unhinged and released from all earthly forms, including passacaglias.

There are only a very few great Wagnerian sopranos who can sing Isolde. And the reason that there are so few of them is the nearly impossible demands Wagner makes on the human voice. "I don't care if it is impractical or even impossible," says the composer, "this is what *I* want." Romanticism with a capital I: I, the artist. And so the performer now had to match the creator in his excesses, which resulted in the phenomenon of the divine actress, the matinee idol, the glorified ballerina, the orchestra conductor, and especially the instrumental virtuoso: Chopin, at whose recitals grown men were reduced to tears; Liszt, whose piano-playing caused ladies to swoon; and Paganini, who played with ease and brilliance music of such impossible difficulty—including his own—that it was said he had sold his soul to the devil—in fact, that he might even *be* the devil. And, of course, there is the operatic diva.

Soprano, with orchestra, sings the "Liebestod" *from* Tristan und Isolde:

Im - mer lich - ter   wie _____   er leuch - tet

By now we have some general idea of the fiery spirit of the romantic period. It amounted almost to a new religion, this fanatic new
cult of the individual, with the artist as priest and prophet, officiat-
ing at the high altar of humanism. As Pushkin said in his famous
poem to the poet: "You are the Czar!" You, the artist, are the real
sovereign, through the strength of your divine imagination. There
is no greater power on earth.

But now let's find out how the actual *techniques* of music
were affected by this new wave. I am sure you have already
sensed that the essence of the whole movement is freedom, individual freedom, which for our purposes we can break up into four
freedoms (to borrow a famous phrase), four musical freedoms
that were the romantic composer's articles of faith.

The first is freedom of tonality. I'm going to assume, hopefully,
that you know what tonality means, that sense of a root, or center,
or home base, located in one of the twelve different tones out of
which our Western music is made, one specific tone to which all
the other eleven tones are related and dependent. For example, if
that home tone, or tonic, is F:

L.B. at the piano:

there arises from it a scale of six other tones that belong to the
key of F:

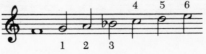

And we're back to F again:

This is called a diatonic scale; and as long as we make music using only the seven notes of that scale, we have diatonic music, in the key of F:

But what about the other five notes, like this B natural:

or this F sharp:

which don't belong to the key of F at all? Are they to be excluded from any music in the key of F? Ah, that's where the subject of freedom comes in. You see, the tyranny of classical times set up a great system of laws regarding these dissonances, these non-F foreigners, laws that prescribed very careful treatment indeed for their use, like Alien and Sedition Acts. And this was the system that the nineteenth century inherited—the stability of a firm tonal system. It was comfortable and safe and formalized, like the painting by Fragonard. But comes the Romantic Revolution, comes the new personal artist crying, "Me! Me! Me!" and the old tonal tyranny begins to totter.

From Beethoven in 1800 to Mahler in 1900, the whole nineteenth century is one long record of the battle to free those poor non-F tones from their legal tyrannies. In musical terms we say that music became more and more *chromatic;* that is, the smaller intervals between the notes of a diatonic scale:

began to be used more frequently and more freely, in the name of
self-expression. The word *chromatic* itself suggests the metaphor; it
is as if the palette of colors between one end of the F spectrum and
the other had been enriched by the addition of these inner shades, a
chromatic scale of *twelve* notes. Whereas using the notes of the
diatonic scale is like working with basic colors only:

Red,   Orange,   Yellow,   Green,   Blue

using the half tones freely:

Red,   Chinese Red Orange,   Apricot   Yellow,   Green,   Turquoise Blue

provides a far richer palette. It's this chromatic scale that makes
Rimsky Korsakov's bumblebee fly, of course:

And think what this new freedom does for the old classical *harmony!* Suddenly we can have brand new chords:

—rich, luscious, what we have come to call "romantic." Do you see
what is happening to the old tonality? It is acquiring a new romantic

ambiguousness, a new subtlety. For example, take this perfectly classical chord:

Where do you feel it must go? To this, naturally:

But not necessarily. It can go here instead:

In other words, that originally classical chord has now become ambiguous. Now, if ambiguity strikes you as a bad thing for music, you're simply not a romantic at heart. Ambiguity means elusiveness, mystery, shifting sands—all of which, of course, fascinated the romantic composers. And if you're looking for shifting sands, you can't do better than a melody by that feverish arch-romantic, Berlioz. This tune, from his dramatic symphony "Romeo and Juliet," paints a moody night scene of Romeo alone in the Capulet garden:

In the first four phrases of this melody, which is in the key of F, conveniently enough, there are roughly sixty melody notes, of which about twenty (marked "x") do *not* belong to the scale of F. Imagine, twenty foreign, dissonant non-F's in a sixty-note melody. One out of three. Whereas in a typical classical melody, like this one from the second movement of Mozart's "Jupiter" Symphony, the ratio is apt to be one to *twelve*, in favor of the F-major scale:

So Berlioz uses *four* times as many chromatic tones!

But it's just that abundance of chromatic tones that gives this "Romeo" melody its mysterious ambiguity and colors it with romantic longing. It makes a perfect portrait of the sensuous, disconsolate Romeo. Romantic music—romantic *not* because it makes you think of sleepy lagoons but because it is said in a personal language. "I, Hector Berlioz, said this!"

And that's not all he said. All these new tonal liberties and ambiguities were matched by similar adventures in the area of rhythm. And so a second freedom was developed—freedom of rhythm. This powerful musical element had also been abiding for centuries under strict codes of law. But along comes Beethoven—again, as always, the first romantic—*and* Berlioz, *and* Schumann, *and* Chopin, and the rhythmic tyranny totters as well. No longer was the composer committed to one rhythm or tempo within any single movement; he could change them at will, any number of times.

He now began to use *syncopations*, as normally as breathing; he developed the *rubato,* a free treatment of rhythmic flow; and he played hob with classic symmetricality. But perhaps the most intriguing aspect of the new rhythmic freedom is the emergence in romantic music of cross-rhythms—that is, two different rhythmic patterns going at once, as if a band were parading past a church on Sunday morning and at a certain moment the organ chorale and the military march became one piece of rather complicated music. Our "mad genius" Berlioz, who practiced all the new rhythmic freedoms in abundance, was particularly fond of this one; and, in fact, he uses it in that very movement from his "Romeo" Symphony just discussed. The scene is now the great Capulet ball:

Orchestra:

Amid all this whirling festivity, in duple meter, Romeo spies Juliet, and his heart sings out to her, in triple meter:

Then Berlioz actually makes these two rhythms, duple and triple, combine simultaneously, and the effect is magical:

Indeed, tonal freedom and rhythmic freedom in this amazingly original Berlioz symphony make you feel the rich new mystery, the heightened suspense and subtlety that these freedoms have spawned.

(Here the orchestra performs the movement: "Festivities at the Cap-ulets.")

In this movement the musical materials and moods keep changing all the time. Why, there is enough material for four whole different movements of a classical symphony. Obviously we are now confronted by still a third romantic freedom—the freedom of form, of the actual structure of a symphony.

What was a classical symphony after all? A work usually consisting of four separate movements, each molded in sonata form, or rondo form, or song form, or scherzo form, or whatever. But that Berlioz movement is molded in none of these forms. It follows no formal discipline except that of its story line. What kind of form is that? Only one word can describe it: *dramatic.* It's no mere coincidence that he called this Romeo-music a "dramatic symphony," because his chief concern is dramatic content and effect, a concern which was a general symptom of this romantic freedom fever. The arts had begun to interact, and we see music extending its province into all the other arts, especially literature and drama. And out of this grows what we call *program music*—music with extramusical meanings, symphonies with names and stories and scenarios. That is to say that symphonies have now virtually become *dramas,* with the emphasis on their content rather than on their form.

Take, for instance, the "Faust" Symphony, by Liszt. Here is a work in *three* movements (already a departure from classical form) that aims to paint for us in notes the three main characters of Goethe's *Faust:* Gretchen, Mephistopheles, and Faust himself. How is it done? By assigning a certain theme, or motive, to each character, and through dramatic transformations of it, revealing a dramatic progress of that character. Here is the main Faust theme for example, portraying the *old* Faust, mysterious and moody:

Violas and celli:

But when he has been changed by the devil into a vigorous *young* man, he sounds like this:

Horns and trombones:

The same theme in a new guise. Just as a character in a drama appears suddenly in a new costume and new make-up, so do these symphonic equivalents. Listen to how that Faust theme turns up in the third movement, the Mephistopheles movement, showing Faust in the grip of the diabolical force:

Violas and celli:

How ironic the theme has become, how cynical and distorted!

This dramatic method of having a theme, or motto, that runs through various movements of a symphony is called in the trade "cyclical form"—that is, a form in which the material keeps returning in cycles. This, I assure you, could not have happened in classical music; a classical symphony is *pure:* each movement is a precise, separate, clear unit. And then, as usual, Beethoven lit the spark, especially in his Fifth and Ninth symphonies; and it caught on like wildfire. Almost every post-Beethoven composer availed himself of this cyclical procedure in one way or another. Especially opera composers; just imagine how eagerly *they* leaped at this highly dramatic device. You see, an opera had been essentially a series of songs, in separate and unrelated numbers, like the separate movements of a classical symphony. But now, just as Liszt can thread his symphony with a single Faust theme, so Bizet can thread his score of *Carmen* with a fate motive that appears suddenly and theatrically at key moments of the work. And Verdi can surround his heroine Aïda with a theme of her own that creates her special atmosphere in the theatre each time she comes on stage, almost like enveloping you in her special perfume. Do you know that theme? It opens the opera, the very first notes:

Violins:

We next hear it when Aïda makes her first entrance, this time accompanied by tremulous strings that portray her anxiety:

Then, of course, it becomes a major section of her first great aria, "Ritorna Vincitor":

You can see how dramatic it is to have the music and the character linked so closely—especially in the third act, when Aïda has her great solo scene by the Nile.

(*Here a soprano performs "O Patria Mia" with the orchestra.*)

Of course the prime example of the cyclical procedure in opera is to be found in Wagner. In fact, he made it the key to his whole operatic process, by assigning mottoes or *Leitmotiven* (leading motives), as he called them, to each character, idea, and symbol in his dramas, and then transforming these mottoes, combining them, contrasting them, and generally using them to intensify the action.

Even in his comparatively light-hearted, comic opera *Die Meistersinger* the same dramatic weaving goes on—for four hours. For instance, in the quintet from the third act, various motives from the opera are combined into three minutes of pure loveliness, including this theme of the prize song:

Piano:

and this love motive:

But that's not all. Because this opera is a celebration of *"die heilige deutsche Kunst"* (the holy German art) Wagner even dares to introduce themes from his other operas, as if to say "German art is me." Me! Again that colossal romantic ego stands before us, but perhaps never so colossally as it is manifested by Richard Wagner. But look: in this short quintet, in addition to the *Meistersinger* themes proper, we find a quote from the *Walküre:*

and one from *Tristan:*

And there are others. But somehow all those motives go together in a bliss of harmonic unity. One could almost call this a *symphonic* unity. For Wagner's operas *are* symphonic, each act like one gigantic movement of a supersymphony, with voices developed out of motto themes. Curious, isn't it, that the cyclical method, born of freedom, becomes in turn a strong unifying principle, a discipline controlling that very freedom? But any freedom without discipline becomes merely anarchy; it is the *combination* of the two, freedom and discipline, variety and unity, that produces a great democracy or a great work of art. *Die Meistersinger* is such a work, of which this quintet is a miniature model.

(*Five singers perform this quintet with the orchestra.*)

Well, where is all this leading, this dramatic breakup of classical forms, this romantic freedom of form, this whole cyclical business? To the evolution of a brand-new form, a true child of the nineteenth century—the symphonic poem. A symphonic poem is really only a step beyond the "Romeo" Symphony, the "Faust" Symphony, or even the Fifth Symphony of Tchaikovsky, which has no name and no story but is still dramatically unified by a cyclical theme. For once you have a series of movements all bound together by themes in common, you might as well go the whole hog and unite them *literally* into one enormous movement—a symphonic poem, or tone poem as it's sometimes called—a condensed symphony in itself.

Perhaps the crowning glory of the symphonic poem came with Richard Strauss, whose masterpiece, *Don Juan,* is not only a thrilling piece but a perfect summary of everything we have been discussing, every aspect of those fine romantic freedoms: tonal, rhythmic, and formal. And in addition, it brings up one more freedom, the fourth and last, freedom of sonority, of musical color, the actual *sound* of the notes you hear. In this field, especially where the symphony orchestra was concerned, the breakthrough was tremendous.

Just think of a typical Bach orchestra, around 1725,

(*Thirty members of the orchestra stand up.*)

then a Mozart orchestra, arou d 1785,

(*Thirty more men stand.*)

and now a Strauss orchestra in 1890—virtually our modern orchestra.

(*The rest of the orchestra stands.*)

And the breakthrough was so great not only because of the sheer size of the romantic orchestra but because of its high virtuosity; every player was now a virtuoso. And so all kinds of coloristic and sonorous innovations were now possible, like the rapid notes at the opening of *Don Juan,* formerly playable only by solo instruments:

Strings:

or the use of such novel instruments as the glockenspiel:

or special techniques, like the famous string tremolo at the end, as the sonorous image of Don Juan's death, painting for us the final spasm, the last ghostly shiver:

Violas:

(*Strauss' tone poem* Don Juan *is performed.*)

The shuddering death of the romantic hero, Don Juan, is, in a symbolic way, the death of the romantic movement itself. Written toward the very end of the century, it comes to us with a feeling of nostalgia, as does most of Strauss' music, as does all of Mahler's music. There is a rueful sense of farewell to the joyous delights of that fabulous nineteenth century. And in the strict sense of the movement, it *was* over. The twentieth century came in like a storm, sweeping away romantic notions as so much Victorian bombast, or Third Republic self-indulgence, or bourgeois pretentiousness. Instead, we were presented with a clean, new scientific century, with telephones and automobiles, radios and airplanes. Don Juan was explained away by Freud in two paragraphs; it was decided that Romeo and Juliet would have grown to hate each other anyway if they had lived; and the Meistersingers were just all too fat.

So here we are in our sharp, clean, efficient, hygienic century, longing for the old one in our secret hearts. It's the truth. Why do we yearn so for Schubert and Schumann and Wagner? Why do we run to the concert hall at the mention of Brahms' name? Why is Tchaikovsky your favorite composer? Because he and his romantic hierarchy give you what you yearn for secretly, what our bright todays and tomorrows lack. The romantics give us back our moon, for instance, which science has taken away from us and made into just another airport. Secretly we all want the moon to be what it was before—a mysterious, hypnotic light in the sky. We want love to be mysterious too, as it used to be, and not a set of psychotherapeutic rules for interpersonal relationships. We crave mystery even while we forge ahead toward the solution of one cosmic mystery after the other.

We are all still romantics at heart. I think that the world, once bitten by that bug, will never quite be free of the fever, the freedom fever by which we are still so hotly driven. But the way we live is no longer romantic; and so, when we are most sorely pressed, we look backward, and we play Schumann:

(The orchestra finished the program by playing the slow movement of Robert Schumann's Second Symphony.)

III

A Sabbatical Report

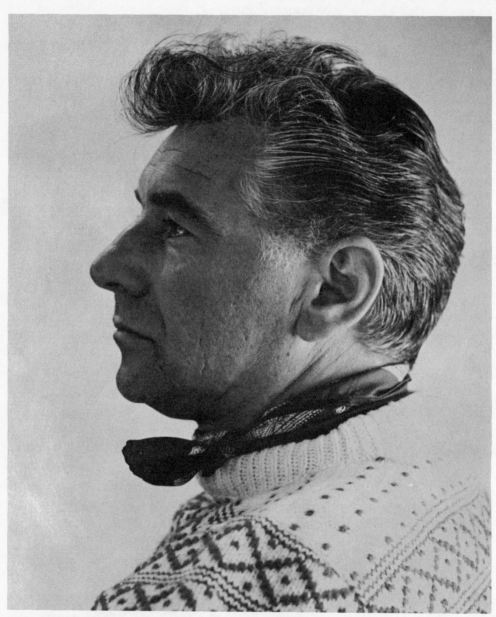

BERKO. ASPEN, COLORADO

A SABBATICAL REPORT*

I

The great benefit of a sabbatical year is not so much that it affords a rest from one's labors as that it provides the glorious luxury of time to meditate, off-schedule, at ease, and without fixed limits. This fact leads people to expect someone who is just emerging from a sabbatical to reappear as newly wise, overflowing with insights, reappraisals, and majestic philosophical conclusions. These I do not have handy.

The one conclusion that I have reached after a year's mulling is simply the ancient cliché that the certainty of one's knowledge decreases in proportion to thought and experience. The moment you have time to intellectualize your perceptions, established certainties will begin to crumble, and the "other side" of any controversy will beckon appealingly. The inevitable result is that one's liberalism becomes stretched to the point of absurdity. It is a Hamlet-like torture to be truly liberal; everything becomes susceptible to contradictory interpretations; bias is impossible, opinion wobbly, and immortal words out of the question.

It is in this context that I have been thinking all year about music, especially about the present crisis in composition and its possible consequences in the near future. What has happened to symphonic forms? Are symphonies a thing of the past? What will become of the symphony orchestra? Is tonality dead forever? Is the international community of composers really, deeply, ready to accept that death?

---

* Mr. Bernstein was on sabbatical leave from his Directorship of the New York Philharmonic during the season 1964–65, and wrote this report for *The New York Times* on his return.

If so, will the music-loving public concur? Are the new staggering complexities of music vital to it, or do they simply constitute pretty *Papiermusik*?

Having mulled over these questions for a year or more, with open-mindedness *ad absurdum*, I naturally cannot provide a single answer. Or, to be more accurate, I can provide far too many answers, all of them possibly true. For each question there are two answers, roughly corresponding to yes and no, and attended by innumerable variations.

For example: are symphonies a thing of the past? No, obviously, since they are still being written in substantial quantity. But yes, equally obviously, in the sense that the classical concept of a symphony—depending as it does on a bifocal tonal axis, which itself depends on the existence of tonality—*is* a thing of the past.

Does that mean that symphonies can no longer be created? No. In a loose sense the word *symphony* can be applied to all kinds of structures. On the other hand, yes. In a strict sense the decline of the symphony can perceptibly be dated back to the beginning of our century.

Then, if the symphony as a form is all but over, what will happen to our orchestras? Will they become museums of the past, with conductors as curators who hang up the old masterpieces with solicitude as to position and lighting? Yes, inevitably, since our orchestras were created specifically to perform those masterpieces. But also no; there can conceivably be any number of new forms of composition that could gradually and subtly change the shape and content of our orchestras. No, yes; no, yes; yes, no. What is really true?

If I may be pardoned for a quasi-existential paradox, I suggest that the answer is in the questioning. By experimenting with the problem, by feeling it out, by living with it, we are answered. All our lives are spent in the attempt to resolve conflicts; and we know that resolutions are impossible except by hindsight. We can make temporary decisions (and do, a thousand times a day), but it is only after death that it can be finally perceived whether we ever succeeded in resolving our conflicts. This is patent, since as long as we live we continue the attempt to resolve them. That attempt is the very action of living. So, in the case of the symphony problem, we are attempting to solve it by instituting a two-year Philharmonic survey on the subject of the symphony in the twentieth century. I don't pretend that at the end of two seasons we will have a pat answer, but we will have answered the questions by having asked them *in music*, by having experienced the survey itself.

I suddenly realize that these remarks are in danger of sounding like sophistry. I hope not. I have never meant anything more solemnly. Let me try an analogy: how should one read a palindrome? The fact that it *is* a palindrome tempts you to read it backward, but don't forget that you have already read it forward:

A MAN, A PLAN, A CANAL—PANAMA!

The essence of it, the whole point of it, is that it can be read *both* ways. And not only can, but should, and must, if its meaning is to exist.

Still sophistic? Think of a great novel—*Billy Budd*, for instance. We are presented with two heroes, two stories, really, depending on how you read Melville's symbolism. Melville himself remains impartial and does not cue you on how to read it, so the sought-for resolution turns out to be the tragedy itself. The ending is a sublime catharsis, but it is not a resolution, since the pain of the conflict remains with us, unassuaged. The same goes for *The Brothers Karamazov, King Lear*, Brahms' Fourth. A work of art does not answer questions, it provokes them; and its essential meaning is in the tension between the contradictory answers.

This kind of dialectical thinking is certainly not new; what may be new is applying it to contemporary musical matters, which suffer generally from overopinionatedness. Consider the avant-garde, with its short-lived fads and "in" groups, its chic efficiency, its cavalier attitude toward communication with the public. One is tempted to settle for a firm No; but with extra time to think and spend with the scores, one is bowled over by the phenomenon of Boulez or by the incredible imagination of Lukas Foss. The No turns to Yes overnight; yet both answers have been objectively arrived at. This is not merely a matter of distinguishing talent from the mass of new composers, it is a question of resolving the riddle of the existence of these two geniuses in a shaky musical moment. And the riddle is its own answer: their struggle is tomorrow's history book.

Of course I, personally, have an added dialectical problem. As a conductor I am fascinated by, and wide open to, every new sound-image that comes along; but as a composer I am committed to tonality. Here is a conflict, indeed, and my attempt to resolve it is, quite literally, my most profound musical experience. And if this sounds far too existential for an old romantic like me, well and good; I am ready to switch and consider the teleological approach, and wrestle with that. Another synthesis to be sought.

Such is the pass to which my sabbatical year has brought me. I have two answers to everything and one answer to nothing. And this lovely absurdity extends finally to writing this very report. There are two solutions; therefore I have written both. And the choice between them lies in the question "Which one is true?," to which there is no single answer.

II

In glad compliance with your request,
O, *New York Times,* that I testify
On my late sabbatical (dubious rest!)
And the fruits thereof, I now comply.
But why in verse? I do not know.
This is the way it wants to go,
Spontaneously. It may be rhymed,
Or not; and tetrametric, though
Here and there I may add a foot or so,
Indulge in quatrains, couplets, or
In absolutely blank pentameter—
Anything, only not in prose.
End of apology. Here goes.

Since June of nineteen-sixty-four
I've been officially free of chore
And duty to the N. Y. Phil.—
Fifteen beautiful months to kill!
But not to waste: there was a plan,
For as long as my sabbatical ran,
To write a new theatre piece.
(A theatre composer needs release,
And *West Side Story* is eight years old!)
And so a few of us got hold
Of the rights to Wilder's play *The Skin of Our Teeth.*
This is a play I've often thought was made
For singing, and for dance. It celebrates
The wonder of life, of human survival, told
In pity and terror and mad hilarity.
Six months we labored, June to bleak December.
And bleak was our reward, when Christmas came,
To find ourselves uneasy with our work.
We gave it up, and went our several ways,
Still loving friends; but still there was the pain
Of seeing six months of work go down the drain.

The picture brightens, come New Year:
The next nine months restore some cheer
That vanished when our project died.
I firmly brushed regrets aside,
And started a whole new sabbatical,
Forgetting all projects dramatical,
And living, for once, as a simple man,
Partaking of life, as you never can
With a full Philharmonic season to run.
Now, here was a project that could be done:
Stay home, go out; see friends, see none;
Take walks with the children; study for fun;
Practice the piano; attend the Bonnard
Exhibit; visit your neighborhood bar;
See more of the people in other arts,
Meet your nonmusical counterparts;
Read the new poets; play anagrams, chess;
Complete the crosswords in the British press;
Restudy Opus 132;
Do, in short, what you want to do.

All these I did; but inevitably
One finds that sabbaticals aren't that free.
There are certain commitments that cannot be
Unmet or interrupted, e.g.,
The Young People's Concerts, recording sessions,
And similar nonsabbatic digressions.
These took time, and a certain amount
Of adjusting,
                    But kept my baton from rusting.
Meanwhile, there lurked at the back of my mind
The irrational urge (too late!) to find
Another theatrical project, which meant
That hours and days were now to be spent
In reading plays and considering oceans
Of wild ideas and desperate notions.
None took fire, which is just as well,
For I then had the luxury, truth to tell,
Of time to think as a pure musician,
And ponder the art of composition.
For hours on end I brooded and mused

On *materiae musicae,* used and abused;
On aspects of unconventionality,
Over the death in our time of tonality,
Over the fads of Dada and Chance,
The serial strictures, the dearth of romance,
"Perspectives in Music," the new terminology,
Physicomathematomusicology;
Pieces called "Cycles" and "Sines" and "Parameters";
Titles too beat for these homely tetrameters;
Pieces for nattering, clucking sopranos
With squadrons of vibraphones, fleets of pianos
Played with the forearms, the fists and the palms—
—And then I came up with the "Chichester Psalms."
These psalms are a simple and modest affair,
Tonal and tuneful and somewhat square,
Certain to sicken a stout John Cager
With its tonics and triads in B flat major.
But there it stands—the result of my pondering,
Two long months of avant-garde wandering—
My youngest child, old-fashioned and sweet.
And he stands on his own two tonal feet.

Well, that was my major sabbatical act—
At least, the most tangible; but in fact
There were other boons from my new-found leisure
That brought me (and, I hope, others) pleasure.
In doing research for this résumé
I've looked through my date-book since New Year's day
To see what I actually did, for fun,
Things I could otherwise not have done.
I cannot go into the bulk of it:
Let suffice one item per month. To wit:

Jan. Conducted Stravinsky's "Histoire du Soldat"
For a benefit. Staging and all. A ball.
Feb. Flew out to Aspen. Institute Seminar
With skiing on the side. Came back revivified.
Mar. Conducted new Robbins ballet, *Les Noces.*
Stravinsky again. Now there's a blessed pen.
Apr. Practiced and played and recorded Mozart
G minor, with Juilliard Quartet. Not to forget.

May. To Denmark. The Sonning Prize. As thanks,
Played Nielsen's Third. A marvel, take my word.
Jun. To Puerto Rico. Conducted before
Casals, musician supreme. A lifelong dream.
Jul. To Chichester, en famille, to hear
My Psalms in the place for which they were written. Smitten.
Aug. To Tanglewood, scene of my happiest youth,
To conduct, on its quarter-centennial, "Carmen," Act IV.
Tanglewood! Twenty-five years! So much to remember!
For instance . . .

         . . . and suddenly here it is, September.

IV

Four Symphonic Analyses

Aus der neuen Welt.
„Z nového světa."
Symphonie
(Nº 5, E moll.)

für

grosses Orchester

von

ANTON DVOŘÁK.
Op. 95.

PARTITUR.

Verlag und Eigenthum für alle Länder
von
N. SIMROCK in BERLIN.

DVOŘÁK: SYMPHONY
NO. 9 IN E MINOR, OPUS 95
"FROM THE NEW WORLD"

Does this music look like the New World to you?

It comes from a symphony subtitled "From the New World," and

there ought to be something about it to justify that title. We are
going to try to find out what it is, if indeed there is anything at all.

Just before the turn of this century a composer named Antonin
Dvořák—a Czech, or in terms of those days, a Bohemian—came to
spend two years in America. Since he was one of the big names of
the time, celebrated as both composer and teacher, every word he
had to say was being swallowed up hungrily. Besides, America was
then at its height of expansion—all fortunes and frontiers—and was
beginning to feel herself somewhat behind culturally. Anything or
anyone that came from Europe was pure gold, especially in music.
There was no such thing as an "American" school of composers
then. An American composer would go to study in Europe, with
Liszt or with a pupil of Brahms, and would then return to his native
shores carrying under his arm a sheaf of fine, academic imitations
of those masters' compositions. If his new symphonic poem sounded
like Liszt or Brahms, it was fine—and the more it did, the better.

Dvořák arrived here filled with the spirit of nationalism that was
then sweeping the European nations. A century of national con-
solidation had just reached a climax: there had been Bismarck and
Garibaldi and all the rest, and there was suddenly an Italy, a Germany, a Bohemia. And there were suddenly also Bohemian concert
pieces by Dvořák and Smetana, Norwegian dances by Grieg, Spanish dances by Albéniz, Russian operas by Glinka and Moussorgsky,
Hungarian rhapsodies by Liszt, and so on and on. You could listen
to a piece of European music and know immediately what nation-
ality it represented, based as it was on the native, primitive folk
music of each country. Dvořák arrived in America an evangelist, a
missionary of nationalism, and he was appalled at the imitative
procedures of American composers. He could not understand why
they were not producing equally nationalistic music in their own
terms. "Look at your country," he said, in effect. "Here you live in a
land abounding in folk traditions and folk material of the most
varied and exotic kinds. What of your Indians, with their noble
chants and dances? What of your Negroes, with their spirituals,
ballads, laments, and work songs? Why do you not create a wealth
of symphonic music from this treasury of material? You have a
heritage; all you have to do is use it."

What Dvořák did *not* know, of course, was that the American composer of the time had no heritage at all. He failed to see the obvious fact that composers in this country were not Indians, and very rarely Negroes, and that furthermore they had little if any cultural contact with Indians and Negroes. Americans were cultural imports from Europe, cultural immigrants, all with totally different backgrounds—and none of them native American. Our *native* Americans were all to be found on reservations—not in the cities, and certainly not in the world of art.

And so what Dvořák was suggesting was that American composers should sit themselves down and write self-conscious American music, based on a folklore that was not really their own. After all, *they* had never gone out to the fields and prayed for rain by beating on drums; neither had they sung laments on the levee. But these composers were so impressed by this apparently simple recipe for a nationalistic American music that they responded with gusto and enterprise. There followed an epidemic of Indian operas and Negro suites that flooded the market, and still, to this day, gather dust in our library archives and secondhand book stores. Such men as Edward MacDowell and Henry Gilbert and Samuel Coleridge-Taylor and Charles Wakefield Cadman, even Victor Herbert (a very *Irish* American), were in the vanguard of this movement. And all this rash of Americanitis was spread by Dvořák's own virus, for he had said, "You *can* write American music, and I'll show you how." Forthwith he wrote his Fifth* Symphony, known as the "New World" Symphony, which purported to be a model of the new American music.

What emerged, of course, is a beautiful, finely wrought and deeply felt Old World symphony. There are tunes here and there that sound Indian or Negro or both, tunes that in fact might have been based on authentic folk themes, although Dvořák has denied their authentic origin, claiming to have written only in the *spirit* of the folk music. But the symphonic music that results from them is Bohemian, or Central European, or Brahmsian, or even Dvořákian, if you will; it is not, by any stretch of the imagination, *American* music.

The American composers who followed his example produced the . same kind of result. If you study their music you find a sort of paste-

---

* Lately renumbered the Ninth Symphony.

job of form. A piece may begin with an "Indian" theme, then be followed by a transition section leading to a "Negro" theme, but the transition section itself is constructed out of the same old European musical fabric that supplied Tchaikovsky and Brahms and Wagner. The same is true of all development sections. So what we are left with is a few islands of American thematic material floating in a sea of European tradition. The land remains land and the water remains water, and they never mix.

Much later on—after the First World War in fact—a real American spirit was to make itself felt in our music as a result of a natural growing up and integration of our society. Of course the great unifying force—the common denominator of American music—was to be a new kind of music called *jazz*. Jazz was to become the true American folk music, everyday household stuff, not exotic and special like Indian war chants, and would therefore become a *real* part of our musical thinking. But in this earlier time of Dvořák, before jazz was born, our American music never got to be much more American than this "New World" Symphony itself.

Now let's look at the music and see how it fits these concepts. Examining the work, one is immediately struck by the great wealth of invention in it; and all of it is effective, whether charming, dramatic, or touching. In fact there is so much material that the piece could almost be said to suffer from lack of development. I suppose that that's the difference between the greatest symphonies and the less great symphonies. For example, Beethoven's actual material in his "Eroica" Symphony is very little in comparison to Dvořák's, but what he makes of that little material is staggering. Dvořák relies more on the effectiveness of his tunes and themes and ideas than on the magnificence of architecture that results from them.

Well, what are these themes? Beginning with the first movement, we hear first a slow introduction:

Now, if this is really going to be an American symphony, this introduction ought to lay it out for us, and strike the "New World" tone immediately. But it doesn't; rather it makes the impression of an introspective, European meditation. In fact, a little later on, this introduction bears a striking resemblance to Brahms' introduction to the last movement of his First Symphony; and this is no accident. Brahms was a great influence in the life and music of Dvořák. Brahms had bestowed prizes on him, encouraged him, inspired him. Here are three bars from the Brahms symphony; notice the dramatic use of syncopation, diminished seventh chords, and the tympani at the climax:

Now let's look at four bars from Dvořák's introduction, noticing the same elements:

The similarity is amazing. We can only conclude from this that Dvořák is more involved with Brahms than he is with America.

Then we reach the main section of the first movement, the Allegro. I suppose the first theme:

could be said to be "American" because of the syncopation that occurs in it:

But it also occurred in the introduction we just heard, and in Brahms as well, who had no New World intentions. This kind of syncopation is to be found also in Bach and Mozart and everywhere else for that matter. Here it is, for example, in Beethoven's third *Leonore* overture:

—and you surely can't call *that* American. So syncopation by itself is not a factor. But even if we admit that it is a factor in making Dvořák's tune American, we find that the next four bars are pure Czech:

so that any American quality is abruptly removed.

This material is developed for a while in fine European style and leads to a second theme:

Now, this tune has been often cited as Indian—in quality, at least—and there are reasons to support the argument. First of all, it has, instead of harmony, a pedal point—that is, one repeated tone—to hold up the tune:

This is typical of primitive music. Later it even has those all-too-familiar empty fifths in the bass that we all associate with Indian music:

Dvořák uses them like this:

Then again, the melody is modal—which means that it is written in neither a major nor a minor scale, as is customary in classical Western music, but in a *mode,* which is true of most exotic folk music. In this case it is the Aeolian mode:

Some Indian music is known to have used this mode. But then so has much early English music and Gregorian church music and Hindu and African and old Greek music. So the argument for Indian quality falters a bit. This tune could just as well be a French medieval dance as an Indian chant. And that goes for the pedal point and the fifths in the bass too.

What is more, the development of this theme follows all the traditional European patterns, so that whatever Indian quality there was is lost. The pattern here is based on the idea of sequences—which means that you simply take a motive or figure and repeat it on ever-ascending degrees of the scale, so that it gives the feeling of building, as Tchaikovsky does in his "Romeo and Juliet":

In this case Dvořák builds his sequence on the second bar only of his tune, and the development comes out like this:

It doesn't sound very different from the procedures of Wagner and Tchaikovsky, does it?

Well, what about the next theme, which has always been compared to "Swing Low, Sweet Chariot," a Negro spiritual that, as you all know, goes like this:

Swing low   sweet char - i - ot ____   com - in' for to car - ry me   home

Dvořák's tune does resemble it, especially if you leave out the first three notes ("Swing low sweet") and start with "chariot":

But Dvořák denied that he had helped himself to the tune. He insisted that the resemblance lay mainly in the fact that both tunes are in the pentatonic scale—that is, a five-note scale typical of Indian music and some African music:

But to those five notes, in the fifth bar of the tune, he introduces a sixth tone, and the pentatonic scale is gone. And in the seventh bar he writes the one remaining seventh tone:

—so that he has now used all seven notes of our good old major scale:

As before, when it comes to developing this tune (its third bar, at least), we are again back in the world of Wagner and all the European traditions:

That is all the material of the first movement and all its claim to Americanism. No, wait; there are those who point with pride to what they say is a quote from—of all things—the "Stars and Stripes Forever." It occurs in the middle of the development section:

If the truth be known, the Sousa march was written three years *after* Dvořák composed his symphony. In any case this would at best be a specious method of writing American music.

We come now to the second movement, which has a charming melody, the one most commonly thought of as American:

This tune is known to millions as "Goin' Home," a Negro spiritual that is not a spiritual at all, but a composed song based on the Dvořák tune. Actually, there is nothing to distinguish it as particularly American, unless it be the fact that it is, again, written in a pentatonic scale, which is as typical of Chinese music as it is of Indian or African. Still, we all tend to think of it as American because of the long list of associations we have with it. It evokes for us the picture of field hands, plantation workers crooning in the moonlight, "Gone with the Wind," what have you—but only because we have heard it so constantly played or sung, in the movies or on the radio or wherever in practically every southern situation. (If we were to put Czech words to it, it would sound fully as Czech as American, or with Chinese words it could sound Chinese.) Later in the movement, when it is played by the horns, it sounds just plain German, in the old hunting-horn style:

The next theme of the second movement is a passionate melody, again in the Aeolian mode:

But, as we said before, *modal music* is universal and does not necessarily mean Indian. This tune is followed immediately by a beautiful brooding theme:

in which the only nationalistic distinction to be found is the rhythmic device known as the "Scotch snap":

Well, Scotland does not help our American cause at all.

A fourth tune now appears, which is rather like an old French jig:

So our second movement ends up with elements that could be called German, French, Chinese, Scotch, but nothing particularly American—unless you insist that "Goin' Home" is a spiritual, which it isn't.

The third movement is a marvel of ingenuity and deftness. This is Dvořák at his very best. But I suspect that he is at his best because he is here dealing with elements that are predominantly Slavic in character. The rhythms in the main theme are not unlike those he uses in his Slavonic Dances:

This is followed by a highly original motive that is certainly primitive in character, but it could be a primitivism from any part of the world:

And the trio of this movement comes out pure Austrian, à la Schubert, and almost like beer-hall music:

Ah, but what follows is the very heart of the Czech spirit. Here the genius of the true Dvořák shines through:

So our scherzo has given us Slavonic and Germanic pleasures, but again, not New World pleasures.

And now, the last movement. In general, I should say that this is the most Slavic of all, recalling Russian music of the period more than anything else. The very beginning is strongly reminiscent of Moussorgsky:

Now listen to these bars from Moussorgsky's "Pictures at an Exhibition":

It could almost be the same composer.

We have arrived now at the main theme:

Again, it is modal, in the Indian sense, and monumentally strong in
the same sense. But it could also be modal and strong in a number
of other senses. And when it is treated harmonically it comes out
quite Brahmsian:

There *is* one spot in the movement where I have always personally felt something like an American spirit, not in the notes themselves but in their handling. It is this passage:

Somehow the oom-pah accompaniment:

against the triplets in the melody:

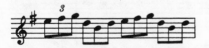

creates an excitement and "punch" that is peculiarly American. But this may be only my personal feeling, born of my own associations.

And anyway, the "American" feeling is spoiled immediately by a
reference to Wagner's *Tannhaüser:*

So we are back again in the German soup.

Shortly afterward there is another spot that seems "jazzy" to some
people. Really it is more like early minstrel-show music:

It is hard to say why this is minstrel-like, except perhaps for the grace notes in the violin part:

It is just as futile as saying that it is American because "Three Blind Mice" gets into the music:

After all, "Three Blind Mice" was originally a British round; and besides, it turns up a few bars later thoroughly Czech in spirit:

That is all the material of the fourth movement, and it is all developed, as before, according to the European traditional patterns. Perhaps a word should be said here, apropos of traditional patterns,

about Dvořák's cyclical procedure—a device he inherited from Beethoven and Schumann and Berlioz.* It means that themes from
the earlier movements of a symphony recur in later movements
in various guises, establishing a superficial unity among the movements and often creating a dramatic effect. In this work Dvořák
has brought back his main theme of the first movement into
the second, and themes from the first two movements in the third. In
this last movement, the fourth, tunes from all three preceding movements recur and recur, to such an extent, in fact, that critics have
said cruel things about this Finale. But perhaps this is because
Dvořák does not seem to be able to finish the piece; apparently he
loves it too much to leave it. There is one coda after another, and
just when you think it's all over, he decides to have one more go at
it, recalling still another theme from an earlier movement. And
when he finally reaches the last triumphant chord, he calls for a
diminuendo, so that the work finishes quietly, after all the build-up,
as though he were loath to call it a day.

The final possible claim for the Americanism of the "New World"
Symphony is that at the very end of the piece a boogie-woogie (!)
bass is heard:

---

* Cf. "Romanticism in Music," pp. 111–136.

Of course this is nonsense, but no more nonsense than the thesis that this bass is really quoting "I'll Be Down to Get You in a Taxi, Honey."

Well, there you have it—a New World symphony from the Old World, full of Old World tradition. Let's enjoy it as a fine, moving European composition, but let's not expect it to be American or to point the way for American composers. For that we must jump a quarter of a century of history to Gershwin and Copland and Harris. But that would be a whole other discussion.

TCHAIKOVSKY: SYMPHONY NO. 6 IN B MINOR, OPUS 74 "PATHÉTIQUE"

Now *there* is a melody, a pure orchestral song, known and loved to the outermost reaches of the civilized world. In fact, to many people this series of notes is almost synonymous with the word *melody;* its immediacy of appeal, its rising and falling line, its yearning and resignation—all these have identified it as the essence of late romanticism.

Almost everyone agrees that Tchaikovsky was a surpassing tunesmith, a shaper of sure-fire melody second to none. He has, indeed, provided Tin Pan Alley with much free and lucrative material. But

171

some musical highbrows and the more serious music lovers always ask a pointed question: is Tchaikovsky really a symphonist? If he is so great a melodist, why didn't he stick to writing songs, or at best, opera? What is this song doing in a symphony, anyway? Is it really a symphonic theme? One must answer no. It never gets developed in a proper symphonic way—or in any way, for that matter: it appears as the second theme in the first movement and reappears dutifully in the recapitulation. That is all. Does that make it symphonic material? No. Then is this "Pathétique" really a symphony? Yes. Let us see why.

Actually, if we browse through the work we find that this is the only melody that is not really *thematic* in a symphonic sense; all the others partake much more of the nature of symphonic themes; that is, they are based on short motives, or figures, which can be altered in endless ways to effect a symphonic metamorphosis. They are not simply tunes that you go out whistling.

Look at the slow introduction, for instance:

This is rather a motive than a melody:

—a motive that repeats in an ascending way:

Out of it is born the main theme of the Allegro section. Certainly it is not something to whistle:

Skipping for the moment over the second theme, which we have already discussed, we come upon a development section devoted almost entirely to the motives of the first theme. There are no further themes as such. So you see that most of this first movement is not at all concerned with pure song. We could go through the other three movements in the same way, with more or less the same findings; and it turns out that the symphony is really more symphonic in character than its critics pretend. There is only one "pop tune" in the work.

Well, then, what are those critics fussing about? Why are they so hard on Tchaikovsky? They would answer: it is a matter of *form*, that kind of inevitable formal flow that makes the symphonies of Beethoven so great. In Beethoven, they point out, B flows out of A, and C out of B, and D out of C, in a way that makes you feel nothing else could possibly have come at any one point. Whereas with Tchaikovsky, they say, anything can happen anywhere. In a sense they are right. Tchaikovsky's formal procedures *are* somewhat academic, following the general broad outlines laid down by the German masters, but using those outlines for his own purposes—melodic or dramatic—rather than creating an original sonata form out of the material itself. This is interesting in the realm of the higher criticism, but it does not make his symphonies any the less symphonies. They are only of another category, born of other impulses—more immediately dramatic, more concerned with shattering contrasts, striking opposites—variety rather than unity. And given their place in history, at the peak of nineteenth-century romanticism, they have their own validity.

But this argument alone would not sustain the validity of Tchaikovsky's symphonies. No matter how one argues, there must always be unity—some element of *real* form—the sense of going forward that makes any good symphony a kind of single journey through time. And this Tchaikovsky has, but in his own way. What really binds these four movements of the "Pathétique" together into one unit is the inner relation of all the material, the homogeneity of thematic invention, the brotherhood of themes. There are several distinct elements that unite the material in this work, and the chief one is the constant use of scales—up or down; but mostly down, which is natural in a so-called "pathetic" piece.

I was amazed when I first studied this work to find how much of the symphony is derived from simple scales. Out of them grow themes, motives, figurations, counterpoint, bass lines, and even tunes. Going back to the very beginning, we find that the slow introduction immediately presents a scalewise motive:

ascending scalewise, as we noted before:

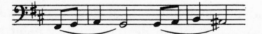

When this motive turns into the main theme its progress is continued by pure eight-note descending scales:

The first climax is achieved by an ascending scale followed by a descending one:

There comes an episode now in which the descending scale is again the controlling factor, alternating between the bass and the treble:

A stronger climax is now reached, using the scalewise motive as well as full rushing downward scales:

When all this scaly fury has finally subsided we are ready for the introduction of our famous popular-song theme. And even this begins with three notes of a descending scale:

The continuation of the melody is also based on scale motion:

Now comes a bridge passage, with more pulse; and this time *ascending* scales are the chief material:

As it continues, Tchaikovsky even introduces a counterpoint in the brass of a slower ascending scale, so that we are hearing scales within scales:

The exposition of themes is now complete, and it seems that we have heard nothing but scales. Actually, it is much more interesting than that, because of the great variety of ways in which Tchaikovsky handles these simple scales.

Now the development section erupts with a crash, and Tchaikovsky begins to develop his first theme:

by making a fuguelike passage out of it; but in so doing he employs as his countersubject—you guessed it—a scale:

This whole fugato, in fact, is built on climbing scale motion:

But at the climax the descending scale takes over:

One could go on this way, finding endless uses of the scale—mostly descending—throughout this movement, but I think the point is already clear enough. Let us note only the ostinato scale played by the plucked strings at the close of the movement as a kind of tranquil, final statement of this material under a brass chorale:

—and so on to the end of the movement.

Now, one would think that Tchaikovsky had really exploited the device of scale to his satisfaction and the hearer's; but no, he has only begun. In the remaining three movements he uses scales constantly, not only as figuration but for themes themselves. In fact, the second movement begins immediately with a charming melody in 5/4 time, built out of simple ascending and descending major scales:

Later he accompanies the already scaly theme with faster scales, pizzicato:

For the middle section of this song-form movement he builds a contrasting, languishing melody—again out of an interrupted descending scale over a repeated timpani beat:

The coda of this movement is almost an exercise in scales: descending ones of a sustained nature in the winds against climbing ones, more flowing, in the strings:

Jumping now to the famous third movement—the great march that always draws applause from the audience even though the symphony is not yet finished—we find scales rushing, careening, whistling, and flying throughout the movement. Here are a few instances:

1) In the very first theme the fourth bar is made of two swooping scale fragments:

Here are those scales in context:

2) Later he uses the scale this way:

3) Now, notice the descending scale that accompanies the new theme:

then, the veritable hurricane of scales at the climax:

and the grand finale of scales at the end of the movement:

If this is beginning to sound to you like a symphony of scales, you must remember that I am picking out only the passages relevant to the point I am making; and rather than condemn Tchaikovsky for his primitive materials, we should admire and praise him for the ingenuity with which he handles them in diverse ways. Perhaps the most admirable of all is to be found in the wonderful last movement, the lamenting Adagio which gives the symphony its *nom-de-guerre*, "Pathétique." It was bold and brave of Tchaikovsky to end a symphony with a tragic slow movement—and perhaps it was wilful and arbitrary too; but it works, and in an amazingly effective way. And one of the reasons that this Finale does not seem like a separate entity, despite its unprecedented tempo and position, is that it is bound to its fellow movements by the same use of scalewise motion. It is awesome to consider what Tchaikovsky could make from the scales practiced every day by pianists and singers and violinists: a dramatic first movement, a gracious and wistful second, a brilliant march, and now this heartbreaking dirge.

This dirge is constructed around two themes, both of them born of the descending scale, which, as I said earlier, is the natural direction for scales to move in a pathetic symphony. The first theme is this:

The second theme is this:

Both themes are made of the downward scale, yet how different they are: the first anguished and desperate, the second noble and resigned. Between them and around them other scale passages abound: gloomy ones, singing ones, plaintive ones. We might quote only the climactic section before the reprise, in which the scales gain speed until they become a whirlwind, much as they did in the preceding march movement:

And almost the last sounds you hear in the symphony are the dying echoes of the descending scale:

Now, I don't want to give you the impression that scales are the only unifying force in this work. There are others, chief among them the fresh and original use of the interval of the *fourth:*

This is an interval that is very common in Western music—almost basic, we might say, since the two tones involved have a strong diatonic relationship:

Think of bugle calls like "Taps," for example:

or the theme from "L'Arlésienne," by Bizet:

But Tchaikovsky uses the fourth in a new way: he builds fourth upon fourth:

or, in the descending version:

—creating a sound that is prophetic of Hindemith and much other twentieth-century music.

Look at this bit of the development section in the first movement and notice the descending intervals of the fourth in the brass:

This has always impressed me as brilliant and daring on Tchaikovsky's part.

But he is not content to use it in only one place; he used these fourth constructions as a unifying factor throughout the work. In the reprise of the first movement, the following passionate section occurs, building to its climax by ascending fourths:

Do you recognize the intervals?

On these intervals he builds his motive:

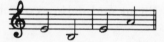

But the real festival of fourths occurs in the third movement, the march. The principal theme is made out of these two intervals of the fourth:

combined in a way that produces the familiar tune you all know:

It is only hinted at toward the beginning with the plucked strings showering sparks of descending fourths on it:

(marcato)

but later it appears as a full marching tune:

First, however, Tchaikovsky has more to say about the fourth. There is a piquant tune in the plucked strings and piccolo, combining fourths with our old friend the scale:

You see how he piles up three intervals of the fourth like blocks, to make this odd sound:

And then, when it comes to developing his march tune, we are barraged with fourths exploding all over the orchestra:

It is as though he is erecting great pyramids of fourths.

One of the more subtle uses of the fourth occurs in the last movement, in which both themes are written so that they lie within that interval. The opening phrase of the first theme:

has a first and a last note:

which spell out a fourth; and the same is true for the second theme:

the first phrase of which lies between these two poles:

again a fourth apart.

One could go on multiplying these examples, but this is enough to establish the point. One should mention, however, other unifying forces in this strange and powerful work: the constant use of the dark colors of violas, celli, bassoons, and low horns in a special mournful way, which gives the work an extra pathos. Again, one could speak of the persistent use of dissonance:

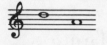

which spreads pain throughout the music. There are many others, too technical to go into; but even what we have studied here should arm us against those attackers of Tchaikovsky who refuse to admit him as a symphonist. After all, the sense of form is a delicate and elusive thing and operates in many different ways. Tchaikovsky's way to unity may not be Beethoven's, but it is none the less valid, communicative, and deeply moving.

Sinfonia eroica

Composta

per festeggiare il sovvenire di un grand'uomo

dedicata

a Sua Altezza Serenissima

IL PRINCIPE DI LOBKOWITZ

da

LUIGI VAN BEETHOVEN

Op. 55.

N.º III.   *Prezzo* **18 Fr:**

Partizione.

BONNA e COLONIA presso N. SIMROCK.

BEETHOVEN: SYMPHONY NO. 3 IN E FLAT MAJOR, OPUS 55 "EROICA"

Simplicity, simplicity itself made manifest. In all the realm of the arts you will never find a simplicity to match Beethoven's. It is a simplicity that shines all the more purely for the intricacy of human feeling that envelops it. For Beethoven, like the greatest of the prophets and teachers, knew how to pluck from the air the essential, the elementally true, and develop from it a complex superstructure that embraces all human experience.

This theme is a statement, a bare fact. Beethoven always started with a fact, an axiom; and his art consists in examining that fact with so universal a range of vision that the axiom becomes living experience. In this sense the "Eroica" Symphony is perhaps the supreme example of that art, and through analyzing it, however briefly, we are going to try to understand something of the great mystery that is Beethoven's dialectic: the wedding of simplicity and complexity.

We begin at the beginning, with those two whiplashes of sound that shatter the elegant formality of the eighteenth century:

Beethoven's predecessors, Haydn and Mozart, also believed in starting a symphony with a commanding sound, a major announcement of something to come. But Beethoven announces something on a scale of grandeur unknown to the others. He is announcing a heroic work, a monument. It is not enough for the rafters of the concert hall to tremble at his coming; the whole world must tremble too. For Beethoven at his best was incapable of making a casual remark; he always seemed to make an important statement. With the most ordinary notes, which in another composer's hands might be pleasant or touching or strong, Beethoven manages to say something important, significant. These two opening crashes of sound may be called merely *decorative,* since they are not strictly thematic; but they make a decoration more on the order of two mighty pillars at the entrance of a great temple:

And what are these two chords, so commanding and brave? Simple triads in E flat major.

The physical laws of music are so constituted that triads turn out to be the chords on which our classical Western music has come to be based. All primitive wind instruments, for example, automatically produce the notes of the triad that evolve out of the fundamental note of the instrument. That is how bugle calls were born. If a bugle is built so that its fundamental note is E flat:

then, by maneuvering his lips, the bugler can produce the overtones of that E flat, and they make the triad. There are only three *different* notes, but they go on repeating in order as the player goes higher:

So out of these three different notes comes Reveille:

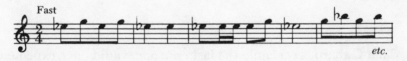

and Taps:

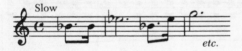

and Mess-call:

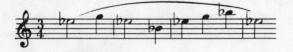

and all the others. And also out of the simple triad comes the opening statement of the "Eroica":

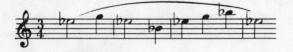

Which brings us back to the big point—simplicity, the basic materials of music. Beethoven has taken a triad, a series of notes that couldn't be more basic, and made from it a theme that perhaps by itself is not what one might call a great melody. The value of the theme is not mainly a melodic one; it lies in its possibilities, its development. It is only the fact, the bugle call fact, out of which Beethoven is going to create his complex superstructure.

How does he do it? By taking this basic musical material and enlivening it, making it grow in oddly new ways, with constant surprises and twists and unexpected discoveries about it. It is this element of the unexpected that is so often associated with Beethoven. But the surprise is not enough; what makes it so great is that no matter how shocking and unexpected the surprise is, it always somehow gives the impression—as soon as it has happened—that it is *the only thing that could have happened at that moment.* Inevitability is the keynote. It is as though Beethoven had an inside track to truth and rightness, so that he could say the most amazing and sudden things with complete authority and cogency.

The first surprise comes immediately after the theme has been started:

That C sharp is certainly the last note one would have expected here, but it is the note that throws the first fresh ray of light on the basic material of the preceding two bars. It is a wrench—an arbitrary, unprepared departure from the home ground of the theme.

What has been accomplished? We have been given the premise of the whole work: struggle. Before eight seconds of music have passed we have already been involved in a conflict; there has been a stab of intrusive otherness; and then we have struggled back to normal within the next eight seconds:

But we now know what we are in for: this first movement is going to be a battle.

Did you notice how we returned to home ground in the section we just covered? There is a crescendo for two bars, and just as we are about to hit the peak of it and land back home on our old comfortable triad, the volume drops suddenly to a very soft level:

This is again a surprise—a dynamic one this time—not of notes but of intensity. We will find these shocks every few bars—there is always something arresting and unlooked for—and each time we will feel the rightness of it.

Now Beethoven proceeds to expand on his triad theme:

But what new shocks have we had now? Rhythmic ones. Again Beethoven is finding new meanings in his basic material. One of the basic elements is his meter: the whole movement goes in rapid groups of three: 1-2-3, 1-2-3, 1-2-3, on and on. And the basic stress is naturally on 1: **1**-2-3, **1**-2-3, like a waltz. But now we are suddenly hit by displaced accents, a kind of syncopation that makes the music go 1-**2**-3, **1**-2-3, instead of the normal **1**-2-3, **1**-2-3:

Then he goes on and does it even more elaborately:

Each displaced accent is a shock, but all the shocks add up to an impetus that is pure Beethoven—exciting, new, and powerful. And all through a simple variation in the way of looking at 1, 2, 3.

This syncopated passage leads us to a statement of the theme by the full orchestra:

and we are now ready to leave this home ground to seek new material, new keys, and new subjects. What ordinarily happens at this point in the first movement of a classical symphony is that we embark on a transition section that will lead us to our second main theme. But Beethoven, the gigantic, presents us with no less than *three* potent transition subjects, each one of which is meaningful enough to be called a theme in itself; and only *then* do we reach the second theme proper. Does this mean that Beethoven is profligate, wasteful of material? On the contrary, each idea is presented pithily, never offering a note more than its potential of the moment, and securely locked into place within the whole structure, like a tile in a mosaic. And so we have a triple transition; but the whole section is less than forty bars long. The transition begins with this lyrical motive:

The second element in the section burgeons out of the first, returning upwards the descending scale that fed into it:

And now the third element (remember we are still in the transition between themes I and II!):

And now we are finally ready for the tender, yearning second theme:

Profligate? It would seem so. Why does he need all those transitions? Let us experiment for a moment and see how the music would have flowed if only the *first* transition had been used. Actually, as you will see, it works perfectly well to leave out parts two and three: the key progression is right; even the orchestration works out smoothly. It would sound like this:

Excellent, you say? Yes; but not good enough for Beethoven. Because he realized, with that divine sensitivity of his, that the lyrical transition motive does not set up the still more lyrical second theme. What is needed is a foil for this yearning—a sense of combat —the struggle we spoke of earlier—in order to point up more dramatically the contrasting tenderness to come. And this is well supplied by the agitated third section, so that when the theme finally arrives it seems clothed in a new, refreshing glow.

But even this contrast is not enough for him. In the second theme we have just heard, the wistful, longing character lasts a mere sixteen bars, when suddenly it stiffens in apprehension, like a wild animal that senses danger, and bridles:

You see how he carries on his sense of battle and conflict? He cannot leave the human condition pat and untouched in this music. There *is* no status quo: there is always the new danger, the all-too-short relaxation; again the challenge, and again the riding off to meet it with a great battle cry:

These elements of freshness are so abundant that it is difficult to choose among them. Take the famous hammer-blow chords at the end of the exposition, the so-called "barbaric dissonance":

Again Beethoven is dealing with a basic commodity of music—tonics and dominants:

but he has channeled a new way and built a new sound simply by combining them simultaneously, to give a sense of pulling and tearing:

Again, in the development section, he is expanding on that first motive we know so well from the transition section:

But not only does he give us an expert treatment of the motive through imitation, as many another composer might, he animates it in his personal way by surrounding the motive with little needling accents in other voices, as though he were shooting this poor lyrical strain full of darts and arrows. They fly from all over: from the violins, then from the oboe, the bassoon, the clarinet, the flute, the basses—from all sides, high and low; and somehow you feel the battle with an almost physical literalness:

In the middle of this raging development, having just concluded a staggering passage of blows and wounds, tearing at us with dissonances and displaced accents:—

—Beethoven does a rather special thing: he introduces a brand-new theme. By the strict rule, the development section should develop themes already stated in the exposition. But the giant in Beethoven takes over again and adds a new, almost elegiac melody, which is like a song of pain after the holocaust:

Again, it turns out that this new material was necessary, to serve as a foil for the return of the original theme:

Gigantic, yes; everything a little more, a little bigger, a little longer, a little stronger, but not one wasted note.

Later on, in the enormous coda that concludes the movement, this extra theme again makes its appearance, again in a most unorthodox fashion, making a coda of proportions that dwarf all others in majesty.

I always feel this gigantism particularly keenly in the second movement—the great Funeral March—where one finds miraculous perfection of form in what seems to be a huge, meandering, slow movement. It doesn't seem possible that there can be so much driving forward motion in a funeral march, especially one that is so elaborate and extended. And yet each time you are beginning to say to yourself, "Oh, now, he *can't* do that theme again; no, I can't sit through it again"—at that very moment he comes up with the most inventive surprise and turns what might have been a repetitious moment into one of blinding glory.

Actually, this happens four times in the funeral march. The first is this (we have just been through the long first statement of the somber theme):

together with all its repetitions and restatements; we have also finished the contrasting middle section, or trio, with its refreshing major mode:

and we are now back to the gloom of the opening. The conventional
thing to do now in a three-part A-B-A movement is to repeat the
first part, add on an ending, and call it a day. But not Beethoven,
never Beethoven. He does return to his A section; but he is only
beginning to tell his secrets.

We are all expecting simply to hear the theme again, perhaps
shortened this time, as is the custom, since it is such a long theme to
begin with. But no, it has seeds of development that are unlooked
for; and so, without warning of any kind, it breaks out into an
astonishing fugue passage of the utmost tension and power:

And again we are caught up in Beethoven's magic instead of simply
hearing out the repeat of a melody.

Then when the fugue is over and the tension has died down to the
whispered hush of the opening, we are once more faced with the

prospect of hearing the whole tune, at last. But what happens? The melody has barely begun when it trails up and off in a wisp of smoke:

—and suddenly, *wham!*

It is the only thing that could and should have happened. Again, at a moment of supposed relaxation, we have been nailed to our seats by Beethoven's crushing force and almost superhuman timing.

Then, and only then, comes the recapitulation of the early material, but varied and embroidered with ever-increasing motion, so that it never stales.

The third great surprise in this movement is in the coda. Beethoven has finally finished all the restatements of the march theme, and we have a feeling of the approaching end. But just at this moment he again injects some of that divine stimulant, goes into an utterly new key, and in the very simplest way, *and* the most unexpected, gives us a moment of such rare peace and radiance as makes us want to kneel in humility and reverence:

And finally, the last time we hear the march melody, instead of a simple restatement, we literally see it break up into fragments before our eyes, like the speech of one so overcome by grief that he can speak only in halting, gasping efforts:

We have just been examining what are perhaps the two greatest movements in all symphonic music. Many critics, even ones who adore Beethoven, feel that the "Eroica" Symphony begins to falter here, since the ensuing two movements cannot possibly measure up to the first two. They may be right in a superficial sense, that almost *anything* would seem anticlimactic after that gargantuan first movement plus the grandiloquent Funeral March. But in a deeper sense Beethoven was right, and they are wrong. With his great sense of timing and just pacing, he knew that the hearer needed relief at this point, relief, at least, from the *quantitative* grandeurs of the two preceding movements; and he therefore gives us now a rather short and driving scherzo, which is eminently fitting. But the *qualitative* grandeur is retained; the scherzo is alive with shocks and tremors as of a deep subterranean disturbance:

What is it that gives this music such a quality of chained power

and pent-up tension? The scherzo is written in the meter of a fast
three: 1-2-3, 1-2-3, 1-2-3. You recall that we spoke earlier of the
natural accent falling on **1** each time—1-2-3, 1-2-3, and so on? But
here Beethoven, by alternating two different chords beat by beat,
gives us the impression of a meter of **2**:

This duple alternation tends to cancel out the triple feeling of the
meter in which it is embedded, so that we are left with a sense of
neither duple nor triple. Instead we feel an ambivalence that tends
to make all the beats equal, as though it were 1,1,1,1,1, and so on.
At this swift tempo, and in so soft and dry a dynamic, the resulting
effect is one of tremendous repressed power, like the first rumblings
of an earthquake. For this succession of equally strong beats, following each other with machine-gun rapidity, conveys to us the feeling
of a series of downbeats, as if a whole bar of music were compressed
into each beat; and it is this compression that makes the tension.
Such compression must eventually erupt, but not before Beethoven
has held out as long as possible, building the tension almost un-
bearably by refusing to release this power. Finally it can hold out
no longer, and the inevitable explosion occurs:

How right, and satisfying, even though shocking, this earthquake is! Again Beethoven is working with his private telephone line to Heaven, with his almost supernatural sense of what must happen when. And this rightness once and for all dispels any doubt about the fitness of the scherzo; it may be shorter than the preceding two movements, but it continues in the same great vein of *qualitative* grandeur and almost terrifying perception of truth.

The trio, or middle section of the scherzo, is based on a difficult fanfare for the three horns, which is every horn player's nightmare. The first horn is led perilously close to his extreme upper limit, while the lowest horn has scampering exercises in his lowest registers, where the horn is least able to scamper:

But Beethoven gives no quarter; the horn players are not to be considered as people but as *instruments*, enlisted in the service of God. And Beethoven's fanfare could never be just another hunting call: it must reach the very heavens, with no consideration at all for the prestige of Mr. Smith or Mr. Schwartz who is actually blowing the horn. So up it goes, come Smith or Schwartz:

There is one splendidly typical shock in this movement that should be noted. At one point Beethoven has distorted the 1-2-3, 1-2-3 meter by his old trick of pounding the second beat—1-2-3, 1-2-3, 1-2-3:

But when this section returns after the trio, he makes one further distortion and changes the meter completely to a duple one for four short bars, in the middle of a scherzo that is otherwise in triple meter:

I call this typical not because Beethoven is given to changing meter in midstream but because it reveals that larger daring, that extra thrust that takes him beyond the limits of every other composer's art.

All that we have said is equally true of the fourth and final movement. It is not difficult to refute those critics who claim that it makes a weak ending to a powerful work. It is actually a finale of hidden power and deceptive simplicity. Is it so hard to recognize this power because it comes from such basic material? Perhaps so. We are again in the presence of the great mystery: Beethoven starting with a bare, bugle-call fact, the absolute essence of musical simplicity and truth, and erecting upon it the same kind of complex superstructure we found in the first movement.

The basic element is made of these four notes:

Nothing can be simpler: it is not even so complex as a triad, since it utilizes only two notes of the triad, not three:

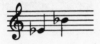

Yet out of those two notes, which are then repeated in reverse-inverse order:

he evolves a series of variations to stagger the hearer.

For Beethoven has written no ordinary set of variations. First of all, he doesn't begin immediately with the theme, but opens instead with a furious rush of sound in the wrong key, as though a raging giant had stormed into the room:

By the end of this raging we have been prepared for the right key—
our home ground of E flat—and the basic theme is stated, or one
might say *understated,* deliberately presented as a trivial thought
ticked off by the pizzicato strings:

Trivial? Perhaps; but only to make the ensuing developments of it
the more amazing. Little by little, tone is added, counterpoint develops, motion increases, until by the third variation we are ready
for those four notes to blossom out into a full-blown melody, which
seems, in its optimism and bright freshness, to belong in the open
air:

And if you look closely, you can see our old friendly four notes,
standing proudly in the bass, holding up the new melody:

At this point all resemblance to the pure variation form ceases. True,
the movement does remain a set of variations, but each one now

becomes a new and extraordinary object, no longer bound to the classical tradition of a certain number of bars, or a constant harmonic pattern, or mere adornment of the theme. For example, the fourth variation, at which we have now arrived, turns out to be a kind of struggle, a roughhewn and somber fugue based on the original four notes, but now set in a moody minor:

By the end of this fugue section, having reached a tense climax, Beethoven suddenly drops us as if by magic into the sweet melancholy of the once optimistic second melody, now sung in the minor, like a regretful reminiscence:

And just as magically it changes to an airy lightness, as though a
breeze had suddenly blown away a shadow:

This fifth variation in itself acts as a kind of shifting-sands transition
to the sixth, which charges in with the dash and verve of a
Hungarian cavalry officer:

Again the old basic four notes are in the bass, supporting the charge.
  This one is a more normal variation, being of the standard length
and conventional procedure. But without so much as a transitional
phrase, the seventh variation begins, the sweet and sunny tune, re-
stored to its major-mode well-being:

And again with the same suddenness, it reverts to minor, as against it the old fugue subject recurs, and we think we are going to have a reprise of that melancholy fugue:

But again the sands shift, the shadows blow away, and a totally new fugue begins, this time based on the *old* fugue subject *upside down:*

The fugue mounts and mounts to a point of exaltation and expectancy of the end; but Beethoven is still not ready to finish. And again, how right he is! He knows now that there is still one architectural span missing that will make this bridge of variations complete and ultimately take us across the river. And that missing span appears now as a slow, meditative variation, which will prepare us for the brilliant coda to follow. Here it is, begun by the pensive oboe:

The climax is reached in the full, final, brave statement of the outdoor melody, with Messrs. Smith, Schwartz & Co. having their great moment in the horn department:

Now the music dies away, again with a sudden cloud of melancholy, leaving us suspended and anxious:

And into this suspenseful vacuum rushes the wild opening material again, only this time not furious but in high animal spirits, and chases away all clouds, all shadows, all melancholy, moodiness, struggle, and somberness, clearing the air for the brilliant, joyous coda that will conclude this heroic work:

The study of the "Eroica" is a lifetime work, and we have only been skimming. But if we can take away with us even the tiniest idea of what is operating in this music that makes it so greatly superior to other music of its epoch, then we shall be taking away a great deal. We have seen something of how Beethoven uses basic musical materials and infuses them with new life; how he makes complexity of simplicity; how he uses the surprise element with that inevitable sense of justness; how his statements always evolve in the large, giantlike. There is hardly a bar in the symphony where these qualities do not abound, and if you watch for them as you listen to the work you will find that you are coming much closer to Beethoven's aims and methods than if you simply follow a road map of the themes. And the better you know this music, the more you will be filled with wonder and gratitude for this great spirit that grappled all his life with the most elemental phenomena of our universal experience.

Vierte
SYMPHONIE
(E moll)
für
Großes Orchester
von
JOHANNES BRAHMS.
Op. 98.

PARTITUR.

Entd Stats Hall.

Verlag und Eigenthum für alle Länder

von

N. SIMROCK in BERLIN.

1886.

Lith Anst.v.C.G.Roder, Leipzig

BRAHMS: SYMPHONY NO. 4
IN E MINOR, OPUS 98,
(MOVEMENT I)

Brahms' Fourth Symphony in E minor is today generally acknowl-
edged to be a mighty work, passionate, lyrical, highly communicative, and deeply satisfying. But this evaluation has not always
been accepted. At one time all Europe was fighting the battle of
Brahms versus Wagner, and musical authorities in the highest places
were fond of debunking Brahms as a dull, dry, thick, impotent,
uninventive example of self-inflated mediocrity. How can it be that
this musical giant, so adored in our time, so warm, so human in his
directness of appeal—how can it be that this beloved Brahms can
once have been so maligned? It's true. Let me offer you a short
passage of criticism by another composer of Brahms' time and place
—Hugo Wolf, writing in the Vienna *Salonblatt*, 1866:

He [Brahms] never could rise above the mediocre. But such nothingness,
hollowness, such mousy obsequiousness as in the E minor symphony has
never yet been revealed so alarmingly in any of Brahms' works. The art
of composing without ideas has decidedly found in Brahms one of its
worthiest representatives. Like God Almighty, Brahms understands the
trick of making something out of nothing. Enough of this hideous game!

And Hugo Wolf was not alone. Tchaikovsky's diary contains scur-
rilous words on the subject; and we have only to look at old copies

of the New York *Post,* the *Musical Courier,* the London *Saturday Review,* or the Boston *Traveler* to find an indictment of Brahms. And with an overwhelming consistency they all agree on one basic fault: lack of invention. Poor, blind people! How could they not see that invention is the very substance of all Brahms' greatness? As a matter of fact, Hugo Wolf inadvertently put his finger on the key to the whole problem when he said that Brahms knew the trick of creating something out of nothing. For that is exactly what Brahms did—well, not out of *nothing,* to be accurate; that, in Wolf's words, is reserved for God Almighty. But out of *almost* nothing—out of ideas and themes that in themselves may seem uneventful but that turn out to be loaded with symphonic dynamite. That Brahms could do this is reason for the highest praise, not for condemnation. How could Brahms' critics have missed this fact, reared as they were on the symphonic procedures of Beethoven? Hadn't they learned yet from the great works of Beethoven that "almost-nothing" can evolve into musical structures of incredible power and beauty? Hadn't they shared in the experience of the first movement of Beethoven's Fifth and watched in awe as three G's and an E flat grew and grew, danced and played and fought and struggled until a monument had arisen? Hadn't they learned that a great musical spirit like Beethoven's could take something as unpromising as a repeated E, in the Seventh Symphony, and build a glorious slow movement out of it? Didn't they know that a Greek temple is built out of dull blocks of stone, and that the ultimate beauty of the structure does not depend on the beauty of each separate block but on the imagination, the dream, that dictates how the blocks are to be put together? *That* is the real invention—not just the invention of a tune, or a chord, or a bit of flossy orchestration. Beethoven and Brahms were *symphonists* —gifted with the powers of symphonic invention, of musical architecture.

So much for Hugo Wolf and his pals. Our concern here is to find out how Brahms goes about this strange and difficult job of symphonic invention, how he creates "something out of nothing." Actually, we are asking the old basic question: what is a symphony? What is the nature of a symphony? What makes a symphony symphonic?

I'm sure that by this time you have all been told over and over again what a symphony is: first, that it is a musical *form*. That is correct. It is an orchestral sonata. Then you undoubtedly know that it is classically in four movements, the first of which is an allegro in sonata form. That is also correct. You are aware that this first sonata movement is normally followed by a slow songlike movement, then by a playful three-part movement called a scherzo, and finally by a brilliant finale, usually in rondo form. All these facts are also correct. You probably even know by rote the essential breakdown of the sonata-form first movement: the two contrasting themes, connected by a transition section, that form the so-called exposition; the development section, in which these themes are metamorphosed and transmogrified in all kinds of ways; the recapitulation, or reprise of the exposition; and the coda, or concluding section, which ties it all up in a neat package.

All this is correct; but all this doesn't begin to let you in on the symphonic secret. And that secret lies in the understanding of the word *development*. Once you are aware of how music is developed —how these blocks of stone are arranged and rearranged—then you can begin to appreciate the building process that is the essence of the symphonic idea; only then will you begin to know what a symphony is.

Well, let's attack the music itself and see what we find. I propose a leisurely voyage through the first movement of this E minor symphony, stopping constantly to observe and enjoy the wonders to be found in it and examining the threads of development as Brahms weaves them into a symphonic texture. Our journey begins, without introduction or preliminary fussing, with a simple statement of the main theme by the violins:

Now, this melody is distinguished by several characteristics, all of them providing clues to the nature of the whole work to follow.

There is first of all the passionate lyrical quality arising from the use
of the minor mode itself, plus the peculiar rhythmic palpitation of
the theme, consisting as it does of a series of two-note groups separated by little rests, or breathing pauses:

We are given the impression of a breathlessness, a sort of panting,
that betokens some kind of emotional agitation. But there is another
quality controlling this agitation—classical symmetry, which manages
to contain the passion in a mold. Can you hear the symmetry? It's
as though whatever Brahms does on the left he must immediately
repeat on the right, like a series of questions and answers, or
balancing weights:

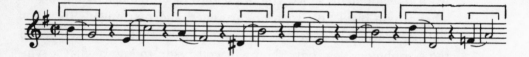

Then there is the fact that each of these two-note groups begins on
the weakest part of the measure, the last little beat; and this further
helps the feeling of agitation—since you get a pulse exactly where
you least expect one—off the beat, almost like a syncopation:

The passionate quality is also bolstered by the accompaniment, made by the lower strings playing wide-range arpeggios:

which gives a sense of surging waves, one after another—to say nothing of the syncopated offbeats in the woodwinds, which lend even further agitation:

Did you notice that these woodwind offbeats are in themselves a version of the violin melody? They follow literally the note pattern of the theme:

—displaced only to make a rhythmic figuration:

So we already have—from the very first bar of the piece—a kind of thematic development going on. This is the first ray of light illuminating the secret we are after—development. We know that we are in symphonic waters the moment this theme begins.

The theme has yet another way of telling us that it is ushering in a symphonic expression in that it does not pose as a *tune*—a complete song-melody—but rather as an incomplete melodic line, which is what a theme really is. A theme *has* to be incomplete—open at the ends, so to speak—so that it requires development, begs for it, in fact, to give it fulfillment. A self-sufficient, closed melody, like "Liebestraum," for example, would not need this kind of development, since it is satisfying in itself and therefore doesn't require the symphonic outgrowth to follow. Perhaps that is why so many people find symphonic music difficult—because they are not getting what they expect. The trick is simply not to expect "Liebestraum"—a full-blown, spun out, complete tune—but incomplete ones, like this melody of Brahms', which has a *symphonic* nature, pregnant with potential. See how he continues the melody, adding this new germ:

and then immediately this one:

which is a rhythmic development of the first motive:

—a development achieved by doubling its speed:

This device is called *diminution* in the jargon of the musical world. Then there are these two other contiguous elements added:

and:

The whole theme is only the combination of all the foregoing elements together, each of which begs for full realization through development:

Do you see now what a symphonic theme is—how many seeds have already been planted for future growth? And this growth begins immediately, with a repetition of the theme, but already with new wrinkles. The violins still carry the melody which is however now broken into octave leaps:

Against it the violas and the woodwinds are toying with new figurations, like embroidery:

As you can see from the encircled notes, this embroidery is really another development, through scalewise connections, of the opening eight notes of the symphony. And what is more, the bass line is playing the same eight notes, transposed a fifth down, *on the offbeats*, as the woodwinds did earlier:

All this together makes a restatement of the theme that is in itself a development of it:

Now Brahms takes the second germ motive:

and begins to feel out the possibilities that lie in it. And here we start to be aware of another kind of developmental technique, that of searching out new keys, or tonalities, in which the theme can be seen from new angles:

Now a new development of that same figure, this time through a rhythmic change. What was this:

has suffered a rhythmic displacement of accent, so that the phrase begins on the offbeat, like a syncopation:

Do you see how this heightens the intensity of the melody? Through this simple rhythmic device Brahms has breathed a new passion into an already passionate melody:

And finally this restatement of the theme develops that motive of diminution we spoke of before:

answering it in the bass:

and then by a *double* diminution—in other words, by making it go *four* times as fast as at first:

Now here is that whole brief development of the theme, with all the features we have noted:

Now, think of it: we have so far had only 44 bars of music—fairly quick bars, at that—of only two beats apiece, and in that short space we have already witnessed development of the first theme through rhythmic displacement, key change, diminution, double diminution, embroidery, imitation, syncopation—a staggering array showing enough inventiveness for a whole symphony. And it is all still concerned with one theme, the first theme; we are now only at the transition section, which will carry us forward to a new key, in which the second theme will be stated.

This transition section contains new germinal motives significant enough to be called themes in themselves; but, more important, no sooner do they appear than they are already undergoing some kind of development, just as the first theme did. You see, that's what a symphonic mind like Brahms' is like; it immediately spots the possibilities in any given group of notes and exploits them to the hilt, just as a great novelist develops the possibilities of his characters through every word they utter.

The first motive of the transition section is based on a descending scale:

which is going to be very important in themes to come, as you will see. But as it appears here, it is already developed through the device of a *canon*—that is, it is immediately imitated by another orchestral voice:

Now the second motive of the transition section—a kind of tragic fanfare:

which is also going to figure prominently throughout the development of the movement. In this fanfare you may have noticed a new rhythm, strongly pronounced and almost balletic:

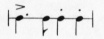

Almost like a tango, isn't it? Well, Brahms now takes this rhythmic germ and makes out of it the accompaniment of the next transitional theme:

And over this strong rhythm the cellos and horns sing out a big romantic tune:

so that all together it really does sound like some sort of huge, mad, German tango:

This leads us back to the fanfare again, now developed through change of key:

Now, taking only those last two notes:

Brahms builds a whole new section out of them, using the pizzicato strings and the woodwinds as antiphonal choirs:

That is real musical architecture—taking the last fragment of one section and creating the succeeding one out of it. But what is so special, and so typical of this great symphonic mind, is that this new section is at the same time a development of the very first theme, which, if you remember, also went in groups of two notes:

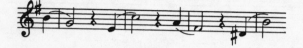

So that when this section occurs, born of a whole other germ, it automatically, perhaps unconsciously, develops the first theme as well:

You see how deep the wells of genius are. Everything connects and is unified at the deepest level: it is all one, just as *War and Peace*, with all its mass of material and events and characters, is all one.

Now the transition section concludes, with two restatements of that descending scale we heard before:

First we hear it syncopated in the winds, with the pizzicato strings underneath:

and then immediately, in a dotted rhythm, by the strings, which burst out of their pizzicato chains, released and free:

This last version of the descending scale is again in anticipation of themes to come; it is a shadow cast before by the coming event. Because in the second theme, which is only now about to be heard, this same scale, in the dotted rhythm, will be used as an integral part of the theme itself; so that, amazingly enough, we can say that the second theme has actually been developed even before it has been stated! These are the intricacies of the symphonic concept—

wheels within wheels, all part of one great machine. Here is that second theme:

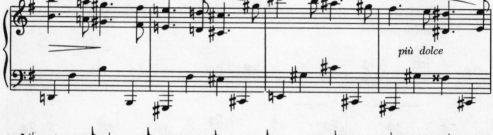

Do you see how symphonically this simple tune is constructed? It begins quietly, like entirely new material:

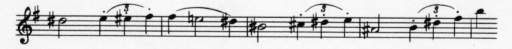

but as it continues it employs the descending scale we have already heard:

which is then repeated a tone higher:

Following this, Brahms, in true symphonic style, takes the last two-note fragment of the scale and develops it in a descending sequence:

making it not just a tune but a self-developing tune, which is the essence of growth in a symphony.

At the bottom of this descent we have arrived at a mysterious moment, with distant trumpet calls ushering in a development of those fanfares we heard before in the transition, but which now approach nearer and nearer as they grow to climactic proportions:

And so the exposition, having stated, restated, and developed all
the material of the movement, concludes with a reference to the very
opening theme, which returns us temporarily to our home key of
E minor, from which we have strayed during our wanderings in the
second-theme department:

And this brings us at last to the development section proper!

Now, it seems almost redundant to call this *the* development section, since we have had so much development already. No theme or
thematic fragment so far has been stated without being somehow
or other developed; and yet now Brahms is ready and eager to
plunge into a whole new development section in which he will show
us still deeper qualities inherent in his themes, just as the novelist
shows us his characters in ever-changing, always new lights.

The development begins where the exposition left off, treating of
the opening theme. We hear it first exactly as it was heard in the
opening of the movement, as though this were going to be a literal
repeat of the exposition, as used to be the custom with Mozart and
Beethoven—but no, there's a difference, a harmonic difference.
Whereas in the exposition the harmony was agitated and passionate:

it is now calm and pastoral:

This character in the novel has undergone a visible change. The development is further aided by diminution; the phrase becomes compressed and condensed:

This compressed phrase now turns into the embroidery of the next section as if by magic:

Symphonic sleight of hand, that's what it is. Because, as you can see from the encircled notes, this very embroidery is made out of the original opening notes of the movement! And what is it embroidering? Another version of the very same first theme, in which those famous two-note groups we noted before:

have now expanded into three-note groups:

You can see that this is the same theme whether it goes in groups of two notes or of three. It is only another version of the original, an expanded, more abundant version. And coupled with the embroidery, which is also a flowering of the same branch, we feel a true development, a sense of increase and growth:

And now we see even a further growth, through a *dynamic* increase, as the orchestra bursts into a roaring, all-out development of those three-note groups:

Now, *that's* development—not only in a dynamic sense but harmonically, contrapuntally, rhythmically, dramatically. Also, it's a bit
complicated. For instance, did you notice that a canon was going
on? A three-note group up high, imitated immediately by a three-

note group in the bass, making a canon:

But did you notice also that the imitation is always a mirror reflection of the thing it's imitating? Where the upper three notes *descend:*

the lower three notes ascend:

And vice versa:

This is called a canonic *inversion*—there's a good term to toss off at your next dinner party. And it's so easy to understand—simply a canon where the imitation is upside down. But in addition there is simultaneously an *uninverted* canon going on, all in the high register —an exact imitation, like an echo:

And added to all these canonic goings-on, the horns and wood-winds are enjoying a wholly separate canon of their own:

based on the embroidery we heard a moment ago:

which was in turn an outgrowth of that compressed phrase—re-member?

—which was in turn a development of this original germ:

As we said before, wheels within wheels. And this canon too is inverted: while the horns play:

the woodwinds imitate upside down:

But the real development is still to come. Incredible as it seems, Brahms has by no means exhausted the potential of those seeds he planted in the exposition. This exciting section of canons we just finished lands us in a new area of sudden quiet, of an almost mystic stillness, where the fanfare theme has been taken away from the brass and given to hushed strings and winds, in an atmosphere no longer of assertiveness but of eerie suspension:

And into this suspended atmosphere the winds recall the opening motive as a two-note group:

then as a three-note group:

then in an even more expanded way:

On through key after key this development goes, finally combining
with the fanfare itself:

Did you see how the two themes finally came together, the horn
playing the two-note group:

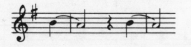

as the winds played the fanfare?

Again, this is development along the lines of a novel, where two characters about whom we have already learned a great deal finally meet, and a new situation is created. It is this new situation, this crisis, that catapults the next sequence into action, as if the meeting of these two characters had set off a sudden violent chain of events:

Real drama. The chain of events has culminated, as you have just seen, in this climactic triplet figure:

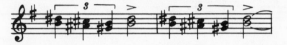

and out of it, in the sudden quiet, Brahms fashions a variation of the opening tune. Variations, of course, are among the leading devices of development, since by definition their function is to re-examine any given theme from a new point of view. Thus the opening motive:

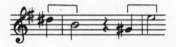

gets married to that climactic triplet figure, and the variation is born. But just in case you miss the connection, Brahms has supplied clarifying clues in the pizzicato strings and flutes, which actually outline the theme in its original form, on the offbeats:

All together it sounds like this:

Now the second germ of the theme:

gets a going-over, modulating from key to key, and finally returning us to the home key of E minor, where the recapitulation, or reprise, can finally take place:

And here we are, back home, ready for the rehearing of the exposition according to the rules of sonata form. But Brahms is not content to abide by so bald a procedure; he has one more developmental card up his sleeve. And so he begins the recapitulation not literally but with the opening theme greatly expanded in time, occupying a period three times as long as it originally did. This is development through what is called *augmentation*—the exact opposite of diminution, mentioned before, which he has already used several times. And so the theme now sounds like this:

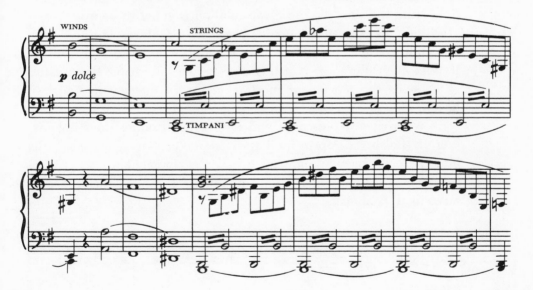

How awesome this statement is! You can't explain it away simply through a word like *augmentation;* so technical a term never explains anything. It is awesome because of how Brahms uses it, where and when he uses it—at precisely the right moment, with a spaciousness of orchestration, with those mysterious woodwind octaves arriving at such a vibrant resolution, with the strings murmuring and the tympani trembling underneath. And so Brahms has not just begun a reprise but has sneaked us into it, without our being aware of it, *through a development*. Always his method is that of change, growth, metamorphosis; and that is the symphonic secret. But once he has sneaked back into the reprise:

he can now afford to be literal, having had so much development right from the start. So the recapitulation is going to be exactly the exposition all over again—germs, transitions, fanfares, embroideries, descending scales, the big German tango, the dotted rhythms—all of it, with one difference: that this time he does not leave the tonality of E, since the movement must conclude in the key in which it began.

So we arrive at the coda; and here again Brahms does not just literally finish the reprise and start the coda, but again *sneaks* us into the coda by whipping up a new development of the fanfare theme into a frenzy of excitement—one of the most thrilling passages in all Brahms:

At this dizzying height of intensity and passion we hear the main theme again, for the last time, at its strongest and most declamatory —and, not unexpectedly, in canon:

As it now continues to the overwhelming finish the various germs of the theme are churned up, beaten, developed to their uttermost limit, almost to the breaking point, as if the characters of our novel were all thrown together in the blazing dénouement of their relationships. They undergo an almost total fragmentation; and by the time we reach the ultimate cadence there is nothing visible but the bloody, tragic battlefield of E minor.

Well, we have had a microscopic look at symphonic method, and perhaps now we can understand a little better what the nature of a symphony is; that it is not just the Jello mold of sonata-form or rondo-form but form in the sense of constant growth, unceasing development—the creativity of life itself.

Which brings us back to poor Hugo Wolf, lamenting that Brahms invented something out of nothing. Are these themes nothing? Far from it. But the wonder is that whether or not his themes are nothing, Brahms *has* worked the miracle. For there is something divine in symphonic growth, something akin to creation itself; and Brahms' critics, thinking to condemn him, have succeeded only in offering him the highest possible praise. Thank you, Hugo Wolf, for showing us the light.

V

An Informal Lecture

"SOMETHING TO SAY..."

The following is, I hope, a literal transcript from magnetic tape of an improvised address given on February 19, 1957, at the University of Chicago. The anonymous stenographer responsible for this transcript has left a number of defeated-looking blanks in her (?) typescript, as well as numerous misspellings, unidentifiable references, and some eerie grammatical constructions. The questions asked during the question-and-answer period, moreover, were evidently largely inaudible to the microphone and have occasionally had to be guessed at. I have tried to clarify the more occult references, prop up limping phrase structure from time to time, and supply the missing bits. The latter has involved a certain amount of speculation and post factum *guesswork, and I can therefore not be wholly sure that every word of the following ramble is precisely what I uttered on that fateful evening. I am sure no one will mind.*

L.B.

I've been seized with all kinds of tremors arriving here today in the plane contemplating this lecture because I've read over the brochure describing the nature of this series and it said something about creativity and psychiatry, and the creative personality, and all kinds of mysterious and wonderful phrases like those. I then asked myself, of course, by what right on God's earth did I dare to speak on this subject? After all, I don't spend twenty-four hours a day as a composer. Therefore I'm not properly a full-time creator; therefore I'm not properly qualified to discuss this. Then, I thought, well, maybe I'm better qualified to discuss it just because of that.

And because half the time I cease to be a creator and switch off that magic little off-and-on switch and become a performer again, perhaps I thereby earn a certain kind of objectivity that I otherwise might not have. At this very moment I have just ended a performing period and started a creative one again, and so the switch went on again last week; but for the last few months I've been conducting. Now the conducting's over and will be over for seven months while I write another show, a rather serious and tragic musical comedy for Broadway*—figure that one out. And so, since I find myself just at the beginning of this period, and having left this long performing period, I think I'm probably just on the threshold of objectivity about the creative process or some aspect of the creative process. Therefore, I thought on the plane, maybe I have the right to say something about it. On the other hand, I'm not by nature a lecturer; when I teach I ask a lot of questions of my students and I like very much to learn from them. The thing that attracts me about addressing groups like this is what they refer to blithely as the Question Period, which follows the lecture. This I look forward to with great lust.

Perhaps a good way to begin would be to recall the question I am very often asked about a practical aspect of the creative process which is, perhaps, a superficial question, but which brings up a lot of others. The question is, "Do you compose at the piano, or at a desk, or where?" Well, the answer to that is that I sometimes do compose at the piano, and sometimes at a desk, and sometimes in airports, and sometimes walking along the street; but mostly I compose in bed, lying down, or on a sofa, lying down. I should think that most composing by almost any composer happens lying down. Many a time my wife has walked into my studio and found me lying down and has said, "Oh, I thought you were working, excuse me!" And I *was* working, but you'd never have known it.

Now, this is a kind of trance state, I suppose, which doesn't exactly sound like a very ideal condition for working, but rather a condition for contemplating, but there is a very strong relation between creative work and contemplation. It's very hard to describe it. People have tried to describe it for centuries. One of the closest descriptions of the state (I should think) can be found in certain mystic Oriental writings. Perhaps you know the little book that's

---

* Which was to become *West Side Story*.

just come out, on Zen Buddhism and archery, of all things, which
contains a rather good description of that state—of the identity, the
sameness of the shooter of the arrow and the target; the identification
of the hitter and the hit. This is a kind of loss of ego. It's something
that I suppose every mystical group that's ever existed, or every
mystical concept that's ever been conceived, has tried to formulate
in some way. And the only way you can really digest this formulation is to experience it, because I have never yet—reading Huxley
and reading the Buddhists and whoever—I have never yet found a
formulation of words that really adequately describes this state.

As you lie on a bed or on the floor or wherever, and the conscious
mind becomes hazier and hazier, the level of consciousness begins
to lower, so that you find yourself somewhere at the borderland of
this twilight area, which is the area, let's say, wherein fantasies
occur at night when you're falling asleep. Everybody has that experience whether he's creative or not. Wouldn't it be marvelous if everyone could consciously, then, preserve just enough awareness, obser-
vation, and objectivity to be able to watch himself fantasizing? If, in
other words, you can allow yourself this freedom of fantasy, then I
think you've hit it. That's kind of the moment you want. And if the
fantasy happens to be a creative one, if it happens to be taking
place in terms of notes, or, if you're a writer or painter, in terms of
words or design—in other words, if it is a creative vision you are
having and you are still awake enough to remember it and appreciate it and know how to go about making it permanent (that is,
when you arrive back in consciousness to formulate the vision into
something communicable to other people)—then I suppose you've hit
the ideal state.

All this sounds terribly mystical and magical and mysterious, and
I don't mean to be any of these things, because I think it's kind of
pompous to talk this way. On the other hand, there is a reality to
it, and it's awfully hard to think of the creative process without
thinking of this almost mystical procedure. So one is forced to talk
this way, even though it may be a little pretentious. I remember
Jung once trying to explain what the process might be. I don't know
if I have it exactly right, but I'll try to tell it to you as I remember it.
He described an eggshell, which is porous, and he called what was
within—that is, the fluid, or egg substance—the unconscious. He
went further; he began with words like *soul*, and so on; but we won't

go into the soul right now. He then promulgated the notion that the more porous this eggshell is, the more likelihood there is of what is inside—that is the really valuable stuff, the essential God-given visionary stuff—seeping through. He liked to call this eggshell the "persona," that is, the outward appearance, the armor, if you will, as other psychologists have referred to it—that aspect of one's self that one hopes is seen by the outer world. In other words, if I have an image of how I look, how I would *like* to look, that would be my persona, as opposed to my "anima," which is inside the eggshell. Now, a person with a very strong ego has a very hard eggshell, which is correspondingly unporous; and, conversely, the less ego, or the weaker the ego, the more likelihood there is of this inner substance seeping through.

Let's say a composer like Schubert had a very thin and very porous eggshell. The stuff was always pouring out of it. He constantly wrote—waking, sleeping, in between; he was always, so to speak, in something like this trance state. His persona, the shell itself, didn't matter very much. He dressed sloppily, he was always a little bit dirty, he was very shy, he couldn't make relationships easily, he was afraid of the girls, he ran hustling around corners at the slightest threat of a scene: he couldn't quite stand up on the outside. Correspondingly, what came out from the inside came out more freely. Now, this is certainly an oversimplification, and I don't advocate this at all. I tell it to you because it is such a clear way to get a sense of the process.

Of course, the next step after this would be toward the age-old discussion of the relationship between talent and insanity, because the thinner the eggshell is, naturally, the harder it is to live in the world—the harder it is to be integrated into society—because the persona is, after all, necessary. You do have to comb your hair before you go to the office, and you do have to have your body covered before you walk down the street. This all has something to do with something called civilization and society. But when the shell is thin we can get to a stage that can be called Bohemianism, so that if one doesn't comb his hair or properly clothe his body before appearing in public, we say he is Bohemian; and we have come to excuse a lot of Bohemianism on the grounds of artistry, and a lot of bad art on the grounds of Bohemianism. One step beyond Bohemianism, one degree more softness of this eggshell, and you have insanity. The

people who lie in hospitals prattling wonderful automatic sentences
are insane. But how often do we hear of people interested in the arts
and poets, as a matter of fact, who copy *these* things down and
present them as real art? True, this isn't highly organized art, but
the essence of it, at least, since it is automatic, coming, as it does,
from a very deep place, even though it's the deep place of a person
with no persona and no sanity and no control. I suppose this is part
of the theory that lies behind automatic writing, that lies behind the
success of a good deal of Gertrude Stein, that may have something
to do with even much better literature, like Joyce and many other
experimental writers. In other words, in this trancelike state, I,
having achieved it, having been lucky enough to achieve it, am not
very far from being out of my mind.

Let's accept that we need this trancelike, out-of-mind state for
anything really important to emerge. When I say *important* I mean
to equate the word with *inner,* with the word *unconscious.* I think
that's the most important aspect of any art—that it not be made up
deliberately out of one's head. If I decide to sit down to the piano
now and write a sonata to be concluded before eleven o'clock, because I have to, and I haven't an idea in my head, I could probably
turn out a sonata, or something short, by eleven o'clock simply by
sheer will. I doubt that it would be any good. If it were any good
it would be a miracle, because it will have proceeded not from the
unconscious place but from the made-up, thinking, intellectualized,
censoring, controlled part of my brain. Therefore the trance is
necessary.

Now, what is conceived in this trance? Well, at the best, the
utmost that can be conceived is a totality, a Gestalt, a work. One is
very lucky if this happens. In other words, you may not know what
even the first note is going to be. You have a vision of a totality, and
you know that it's there, and all you have to do is let it come out
and guide it along. Guiding it may be a fairly conscious process, but
you know it's there. You have the conception—that's the greatest
thing that can happen.

The next-to-greatest thing that can happen is to conceive an
atmosphere, in other words, a general climate, which is not the same
as a totality of a work, because that doesn't involve the formal
structure. However, it is an important thing to have conceived if it
has come from somewhere inside. Every work, every real work of

art, has a world of its own that it inhabits, where there's a certain
smell and a certain touch. Even various works by the same artist
differ if they're really important works. The Second Symphony of
Brahms opposed to the Third Symphony of Brahms—I see different
colors when I just say those names. "The Second Symphony": I
smell something; I feel a texture; I see colors; I have certain syn-
aesthetic responses. It's altogether different when I say "Symphony
No. 3 by Brahms." So that this textural atmosphere, or climate, is a
vitally important thing. From this may proceed, then, the totality of
the formal structure.

Well, that's the second-best thing you can conceive. But if you're
not that lucky, you can still conceive a *theme*. In other words, it can
be a basic, pregnant idea or motive, which promises great results,
great possibilities of development. A theme that is fertile will immediately present itself to you as such. You know without even
trying to fool with it that it's going to work, upside down and backward, and that it's going to make marvelous canons and fugues. You
may not know what I'm talking about when I say things like "upside
down" and "canons"; even if you don't, it doesn't matter. The thing
I'm trying to point out is the fertility and flexibility of the theme,
its inherent possibilities for development. You know immediately
when you get such a theme that you're going to be able to do wonders with it.

This is very different from conceiving only a tune, which would
be, I suppose, the fourth-best thing you could conceive—less important, less desirable to think of than a theme. Because a tune, after
all, no matter how beautiful it is, is finished when it's over. Tunes
can't be developed; themes can.

So there we have four stages of possibilities. I suppose there's a
fifth stage, the least desirable, and this would be, in our famous
trance, to conceive a bit, a harmonic progression or a figuration, a
little design, an effect of some sort, an instrumental combination;
something that will occur to you from which a great many other
things may grow by association. That is the least that comes to you
in this trance, but it may provide a start for something bigger.

And, of course, the sixth stage is that you fall asleep. This happens very often. As a matter of fact, I think this happens most of
the time. Now, the fact that you do fall asleep doesn't necessarily
mean that nothing has happened. Not just *nothing* has gone on in

this "other world" you've been in. It may be that you have conceived some glorious visions and then have fallen asleep because you didn't remain on that border between the twilight and the waking world. I'm sure you've all had the experience of fantasies as you were falling asleep at night in which you suddenly discover yourself in an absolutely impossible scene, having an impossible conversation, perhaps, or doing something utterly ridiculous that makes no sense; but you don't know that it makes no sense at that moment unless you suddenly become more conscious and aware and say: "Good Lord, what was I talking about?" And I am referring now to fantasies, not dreams; not to when you are really asleep but to when you are almost asleep. In most cases the waking up or "coming out" of that twilight moment is in itself a startling little shock, and the effect of that shock is to dissipate the fantasy completely. I know that's what always happens to me. Ordinarily I say, "Oh, what was that?," and then it's gone and I don't know what it was.

This very often happens to you with music, and you pray—*all* composers pray—for some kind of instrument to be invented that can be attached to your head, as you are lying there in this trance, and that will record all the nonsense going on, so that you don't have to keep this kind of "watch-dog," schizophrenic thing going on: whereby half of you is allowed to do what it wants, and the other half has to be at attention to watch what the first half is doing. You can wind up screaming in a schizophrenic ward eventually. Maybe that has something to do with the closeness between insanity and talent.

Having spent that much time on the "trance," let's talk a little bit about the conception. What is conceived? What conditions this conception? What is it that makes you conceive whatever it is that you are conceiving? I should say, first of all, sticking purely to musical matters, the memory of all music you've ever heard before. This is not disparaging. I'm not talking about derivativeness or being imitative of other music. All musicians write their music in terms of all of the music that preceded them. All art recognizes the art that preceded it, or recognizes the presence of the art preceding it. So that it is not unlikely that your concept, the idea that will come to you in this trance, has something to do with music that has preceded it. And, in fact, even those composers who call themselves "experimental" composers (and who are dedicated to the idea of writing music that is different from all other music that preceded it, making their music valuable only because it is different from earlier music) are admitting their recognition of the presence of art that preceded their own, because their art is still being written in terms of the art that preceded it—only this time in antithesis instead of imitation. Is that too confused? Yes. To put it another way, even experimental composers, revolutionary composers, self-styled radicals, are, in writing revolutionary music, recognizing the music that preceded them precisely by trying to avoid it. Therefore, in a sense they are composing in terms of the music that preceded them.

But more important than this, the concept is conditioned by this crazy, compulsive urge to say something. We always hear a distinction made between good and bad creators on the ground that the good creator had something to say—"Something To Say" is the big, magic phrase—and the bad artist didn't have "Something To Say."

"It was a well-made symphony," you read in the papers, "but he didn't seem to have anything to say." Why does a composer want to say anything, anyway? Suppose he does have something to say? Why doesn't he keep it to himself? That is what is compulsive. This is what makes an artist. I always see an image of an artist with a kind of devil at his back, prodding him with a pitchfork. I very often feel this when I am about to enter the stage to conduct—something pushing you out on the stage, an imp at your back. In fact, it makes *you* want to go and look at this crazy thing on a podium, and it *is* a crazy thing. A grown-up man standing on a podium flailing his arms about: nonsense! But something makes me have to do it. It's compulsive. There's no doubt about it. It's maniacal. There's nothing you can do about it. And a composing act is equally compulsive. If you have something to say, you've just got to run off at the mouth. This is something you can't do in private life, of course, because in private life if you have something to say, you have to wait your turn. You have to be sure that somebody cares to hear what you have to say. You have to wait for an opportune moment at a dinner party where you can elbow your way in and say it. If you're a composer or an artist you have this divine right to say it anyway. (That doesn't mean necessarily that it's going to get heard.)

What makes you *have* to say it? It's the need to communicate. All you people here in Chicago are very fond of saying that we are lonely, we are a "lonely crowd," and we are. *Communication* is, I guess, the most written-about, the most discussed word of the twentieth century, and I don't just mean telegraphy. Everybody wants to get close to somebody else. Erich Fromm keeps writing books about how incapable we are of love, and how love is the only way we can obtain any warmth of communication in the world; and I suppose this is the truth. The only thing is that love isn't the only way. Art is also a way. Communication via art. So I suppose you could say that when you listen to a warm phrase of Mozart coming at you, something akin to love is reaching you. Could one go along with a paraphrase of Mary Baker Eddy and say, "Art is love"? I guess one could. I am now throwing you one of those provocative curved questions. Does that mean, therefore, that Picasso is love? Is Jackson Pollock love? Is Gertrude Stein love? If art equals warmth equals love, then Picasso must be love.

Naturally, this compulsion to say something happens in terms of the person to whom you're going to say it, which in this case is an audience. I know that I always think of an audience when I write music—not as I plan to write music, not as I am actually writing it—but somewhere in the act of writing there is the sense haunting this act of the people who are going to hear it. I've many composer friends, and I've read similar documents of composers of the past, who say that they do not sense an audience. These people insist that they are going to say their say regardless of whether anybody ever hears it or not, and they don't care. They have nobody in particular in mind, they have no kind of audience in mind, and they will always point to Bach and Bruckner and others who claim to be writing for the glory of God and no other reason. In other words, the composition of a piece of music is a kind of mystic sacrifice. Bruckner made all his pieces that way. This was his way of making a sacrifice to God. So did Bach. On the other hand, we know that Bach was a highly utilitarian composer. We know that Bach had to get that cantata out for next Sunday, because they needed it. They needed a Passion for Easter, or whatever, and he wrote these pieces and turned out these clavier pieces for teaching, and he turned out fiddle pieces for fiddlers and organ pieces for organists. How do you resolve that little conflict? Another provocative question.

Is this "something to say" emotional? In other words, you can't state facts with F sharps. You can't write music that is going to inform anybody about anything, and, in fact, you can't write music that is even going to describe anything unless I tell you what I want the music to be describing. The "Pastoral" Symphony of Beethoven, if it were called the "Kafka Metamorphosis" Symphony by Beethoven, but had all the same notes, could quite possibly be interpretable as a "Kafka" Symphony and not a "Pastoral" Symphony at all. And the very fact that Beethoven says, "I'm writing a Pastoral Symphony that was inspired by happy feelings in the country, and it begins this way . . ."* doesn't mean that it is pastoral music. What's pastoral about it? It's pastoral only because you've been *told* it's pastoral. Now, what if I tell you that this is the beginning of Kafka's *Metamorphosis*, with the hero, Gregor Samsa, waking up in the morning . . .† Let's say that he feels different, that something's wrong this morning when he wakes up, he doesn't feel quite right . . . there's something different there!

I'd like to go through the whole movement this way and make you a parallel between the "Pastoral" Symphony and the story of Kafka. Maybe it wouldn't work all the way through, but it would work enough so that you would get the idea that you need not be shackled in this music with the idea of "happy feelings in the country with merry peasants gamboling on the green," and all the rest of it. When a storm comes up, in the last movement, and then dies away, and the last little flicks of raindrops fall, and a shepherd's pipe is heard tranquilly announcing that the storm is over and the sun is up, that could all be just as easily equated with the end of *Metamorphosis*. The storm is the crux, and the shepherd's pipe is the aftermath. I hope you get the idea.

Therefore, what it is that the composer is telling is never factual, can never be literal, but *must* be emotional. But it has got to be, of course, an emotion recollected in tranquillity, and this tranquillity is, of course, the half-asleep state on the couch I've been describing to you. I mustn't say "couch"—no. It must be recollected in tranquillity, because, to dispel once and for all that romantic notion, agitated music never gets written by an agitated composer, and despairing music never gets written by a desperate composer. Can you imagine me, as a composer, in a desperate mood, in a suicidal mood, ready to give everything up, sitting down at the piano and writing the "Pathétique" Symphony, by Tchaikovsky? How could

* I played the opening bars of the Beethoven symphony on the piano.
† I repeated the same passage.

I? I'd be in no condition to write my name! This is a lot of nine-teenth-century romantic nonsense that always pictures the creator creating in the mood of the piece he is writing. But that's *ex post facto*. We just look back on it. We see Beethoven writing that "Pas-toral" Symphony while walking in the woods, sitting on rocks, watching the brook run by—out comes the notebook! You can't write symphonies sitting on rocks. You have to go home and sit in your chair and preferably draw the blind and not see one whit of nature, because it's distracting. You have to concentrate on how you're going to get the third voice of the fugue to fit.

It's perfectly possible that while you're sitting on the rocks and looking at the brook all sorts of things are happening to you that will later turn into music, but they don't turn into music at the moment you are feeling the beauties of the brook, anymore than you can write a despairing adagio while you feel desperate. Therefore the emotion must be recollected, as Wordsworth says, because if you're going to communicate with people you have to communicate while in a communicating state, not while in a despairing, tied-up emo-tional state.

The last thing I have to say about the concept (and by concept I mean "something to say," that great magic phrase) is: Who *cares* whether you have anything to say or not? This is a big worry in our time. In other words, how many people in this room give a hoot whether Roy Harris ever writes another symphony or not—I mean, really and truly, down in your hearts? And I don't mean just Roy Harris, I mean *anybody!* Compare for a moment the excitement that is generated by the approach of a new Rodgers and Hammerstein show, the table talk, excitement at breakfast—"Oh boy, a new Rodgers and Hammerstein show!"—compared with the announce-ment that next week a new string quartet by me or somebody else is going to be given its premiere. "Oh boy, a new quartet by ——!" Can you picture it?

Now, this wasn't always the case. Around the time Brahms was writing symphonies in Vienna, the Viennese said, "Oh boy, a new symphony by Brahms!"; and they meant it. And when Verdi or Puc-cini was writing operas in Milano, the Milanese said, "Oh boy, a new Puccini opera, a new Verdi opera!" It was a big event, and it belonged to them; it was theirs. We haven't got that. So, maybe the whole thing is over. That's a question, not a statement.

So far we have talked only about the purely musical aspects of this concept. But there are many nonmusical aspects that influence whatever the conception is that takes place in this trance. The reason I've stuck to the musical elements is that music tends, basically, to be so abstract that ordinarily it operates independently of nonmusical matters. In other words, it's nonrepresentational. A note is a note, and there isn't much you can do about it. F sharp is F sharp; it doesn't mean anything. It's not like a word. It's not like the word *bread*, which means something to everyone, no matter how it's used in a poem. No matter how poetically you say *have*, it still means *have*. And you can see a picture and everybody will see more or less the same conceptual picture. But F sharp—in that there is no conceptuality at all. In other words, it's opaque. Music is opaque and not transparent. That's a possible way of saying it. There are notes, and that's all you hear and that's all you understand, and you can't see through them to any meaning beyond. Whereas with words you read in the paper: "Ike Considers New Israel Policy," you don't hear a poem, but you have a concept; it means something to you. You see through the words; they're transparent.

Of course, words can also be used in an opaque way. If Gertrude Stein writes: "to know, to know, to love her so" or "it makes it well fish," these are not transparent words, since you can't see through them to anything. You are just getting words in the same way that music gives you notes, and if the words are pretty enough, I suppose you can enjoy them for their own sake. But, in the case of notes, it's always that way, *unless*, as in the "Pastoral" Symphony, the composer tells you he wishes you to think of something else besides mere notes.

Now, what are these nonmusical things that come into the picture? Well, the first thing is the viability of the idea. While you are lying there in a trance, somewhere something is going to be censored, depending upon the type of composer you are: your choice of idea, no matter how unconscious it is. Let's call it communicability, and let's distinguish between those composers who care whether they're communicating and those composers who don't care. In other words, these friends of mine I referred to before who say, "I don't care if anybody hears it or not; I sit in my ivory tower and write this, anyway." That's not ever true. Something is going to come from the outer world and condition your idea a little bit in terms of communicability. There are many other outer-world things that condition this idea—for example, nationalism. It was an especially strong influence in the nineteenth century, when it was a terribly important matter to many people, when there were big movements going on in all the arts, with fellows like Liszt writing Hungarian rhapsodies and Chopin writing Polish mazurkas and polonaises; when we had Spanish music all of a sudden (we had never really had Spanish-sounding music before); when we had music that was Norwegian by Greig, and Bohemian by Dvořák; and suddenly there was something called French music; suddenly German music had asserted itself in a Germanic way. All this nationalism is not a musical matter. Nationalism is anything but musical; it is a nonmusical idea appliquéd onto a musical thought; so that if you are feeling nationalistic in any way, it will mean that a nonmusical element will come into your trance and condition what you are doing. In terms of an American, I suppose this would naturally take the form of jazz. And this is the crux of the matter to me. How conscious is this influence or how unconscious? In other words, if I deliberately sit down again to write an American piece of music, I think I am likely to write a pretty bad one. If what occurs to me unconsciously happens to come out sounding American, if it happens to borrow from jazz, chances are it'll be a better piece. This has been proved over and over again, because whatever will derive from Americana or Americanisms will be more integral, will be a more organic part of the music. I could make up a theme that's about as dull a theme as you can think of. I sit down and write this tune and I say, "That's awfully dull and besides it doesn't sound very American." Now, how can I Americanize it? Well, I can apply a little jazz technique to it. Let's say instead of a square rhythm I write the same thing with a boogie beat. That's easy. Now it begins to have a little more personality and a little more interest. I could make it even more jazzy; there are all kinds of things I could do. I'm doing these all very consciously because of a knowledge of how to do them.

I have some friends in the composing world who compose this way, and there have always been composers who compose this way, and there have always been writers who write this way, and painters who paint this way. And they come up with a piece finally that can be almost convincing. Now, let's say—supposing you hadn't gone through that little process with me—I come into Carnegie Hall about to play a piece, a new piece that you've never heard. Let's say I start with a grandiose introduction in Hollywood style, which *could* be pretty impressive in Carnegie Hall, at least to some people. Actually, I've done nothing. I wouldn't give you two cents for it. But this kind of music appears all the time and not only passes muster but causes a lot of excitement. You can always tell whether it has come from an inner place or an outer place. And the people who can tell best, strangely enough, are not the critics and not other composers, but the public. In the long run, the public is a very sure-footed little beast, if it's a beast at all, that knows exactly whether it is getting the "McCoy" or not. Even if they hate the music, they know it's the "McCoy." Even if they are listening to a quartet by Webern and they don't like Webern, they know that it's real, that Webern was a real composer. And the reason for this is that they can sense the communication. They can tell that the music comes from an inner place and wasn't just made up out of somebody's head.

I've got a little list of other things that can influence the trance and the concept, and I'd like to run through it without discussing anything in great detail. One thing that can enter into the picture is a fashionable trend of the time. That's a little bit allied to this jazz business, but it's not exactly the same thing. Again, there can suddenly be a great swing away from tonality or toward tonality. There can be a great swing toward chamber music, toward new combinations, toward writing pieces for groups other than symphony orchestras, toward choral pieces, or toward certain styles. I can't go into the whole thing, but this is certainly a nonmusical matter. There are, on the other hand, real trends as opposed to fashionable trends, and these real trends are part of musical history. The distinction, again, between a real trend and a fashionable trend is a distinction equivalent to the one I made before, between inner and outer.

Then there is the consideration of: What will the critics say? (Something—to be perfectly frank—that may occur to a composer.) There is the consideration of: What will my fellow composers say? What do I have to do to impress them? There is the consideration of: What was my last work? And what sort of work should I be writing now? This is, again, a very external consideration. "My last piece was a somber, difficult, tragic symphony; therefore my next work should be light, something different." Or, taking another tack: "My last work was a somber, difficult symphony and had such a great success that maybe I ought to write another somber, tragic symphony, because that's what I seem to be good at." Or "The critics like me when . . . ," or "The public likes me when I write this kind of thing but not when I write this kind of thing; therefore, I should stick to this kind of thing." Or—just the opposite—"Just because they like me doing 'A,' I will do 'B,' for I've got to bring the public up to date on this side of me; they don't understand . . ." All these things can crowd in.

Then there is the whole business of society and the dictates of social structures. That's a very long story in itself and we can't go into it, but we ought to mention the Soviet Union, where, of course, the most flagrant example of social-structure dictation goes on. I had a letter recently from a friend of mine who is a CBS correspondent in Moscow in which he wrote me an account—very funny, I must say—of a meeting of the Union of Soviet Socialist Composers, Soviet Socialist Republic—uh, I can never remember the whole title—but, anyway, they are the composers' group and they were fighting it out again, that old fight, fighting it out between Khrennikov and Kabalevsky, and the rest. It seems that the oldest guard, who is Khrennikov, has changed his mind. He was always the man who said, "Of course the government should dictate what kind of music is being written, because this is a socialist country and the people have to have the kind of music that goes with revolution and not counter-revolution, that goes with socialism and not with the bourgeois society." Now he's suddenly changed his mind and thrown everybody into an uproar, and all composition in the Soviet Union, according to my correspondent, has been halted until they decide what the new rule is going to be. That, of course, is very extreme, but it happens all the time in the Soviet Union. It happens, of course, in a much milder way in other countries. We are not dictated to by an edict, but we are dictated to in various other ways—by supply and demand, by what a conductor will play and what he won't play, by what the public wants, by what is too difficult, by what is not too long; and so on.

Then there are the influences of other arts, the inspiration from other works of art—inspirations from autobiographies, pictures, books, from stories of other people. All these things can come crowding into the conceptual experience while one is lying in bed. There is also the "trying-to-keep-up-with-the-other-arts" factor, music being always a little behind the other arts. Therefore music has an extra job of trying to keep up with a movement like impressionism, for example, which took hold in painting and poetry long before it took hold in music, as did expressionism. The same is true of the various distortive aspects of painting like cubism, and of functionalism in architecture. Functionalism in music came along about a quarter of a century later. But these, again, are all extra-musical ideas that influence a composer. Then, if he has to write a piece for a specific occasion, for example, there are other considerations. If he is commissioned to write a piece of music for a specific performance or for a specific conductor or orchestra, his conception may be conditioned by what he thinks those performers do best. If I'm writing a song for Maria Callas, it will be a different kind of song from the one I would write for Jennie Tourel. In addition, there are all kinds of little things; for instance, "How much time do I have to write this thing? Only two weeks? Well, then I'll have to write a shorter piece. If I had a lot of time I could write a longer one."

Of course, we're getting down to the dregs; this is the bottom of the barrel. These are considerations that shouldn't ever enter into it, and yet they all do. And there's the final aspect, which is self-criticism, that censor within the mind that says, "Do not do that, it's derivative. . . . Do not do that, it's out of style. . . . Do not do that, it's vulgar." And this little fellow, whoever he is, operates whether you are sleeping or waking if, fortunately, you are a good composer.

All of these things that I have mentioned do operate legitimately in every composer. The difference between a good and a bad operation is only that proportion equivalent to unconscious versus conscious. It's all according to how blithely he decides he's going to put one of his principles into motion. If he doesn't decide anything, he's lucky. If it all happens by itself, he's lucky. If he *has* to decide, then probably he's not a composer at all.

*   *   *

QUESTION & ANSWER PERIOD

Q. Is it true that music is sad when it is written in the minor, and happy when it is in the major?

> **L.B.**
Ah, wouldn't it be easy if that were all! That would really be a snap, because you could say to yourself, lying in that trance state, "I'm feeling sad, therefore I will write in a minor key." But I could play you any number of Mozart themes that yearn wistfully in the major. No, it doesn't depend on that. And then even if it did, you would have a big problem explaining music written in various modes which are neither major nor minor, or Debussy, for example, when he writes in whole-tone scales, which are also neither major nor minor. Would that music be sad or happy? Has anybody a right to divide music into sad and happy? Are those the only two things there are? No, it's not that easy. It's very, very difficult.

Q. Does rhythm or beat have something to do with it, the way it flows, the way it asserts itself?

> **L.B.**
Well, now, rhythm can certainly help assertiveness, positiveness, and lack of rhythm can create a nebulousness, which is the opposite. But, again, you can't divide all music into rhythmic and nonrhythmic. In other words, if you start with a distinction between major and minor, which the other gentleman suggested, between rhythmic and nonrhythmic, which you suggest, between one instrumental color and another, as somebody else may suggest, and you take five hundred of those opposites and make a piece out of elements belonging to all of them, you would still have one fraction of what is to be discussed in any one piece of music. There is a new tendency among aestheticians to stop generalizing as far as works of art are concerned and begin to pay attention to specific pieces and to draw aesthetic conclusions in terms of one piece or another. I suppose that this is a point to which aesthetics had to come sooner or later, because the minute you make a generalization there's always that other piece that is an exception. This is really the trouble.

Q. I have one comment and also a question. Your analogy between the story by Kafka and the "Pastoral" Symphony sort of rubbed me the wrong way. I—

L.B.

I heartily apologize.

Q. I think the short story gives one a feeling of horror that you couldn't possibly get in—

L.B.

Oh, that's absolutely true. I couldn't agree with you more. Naturally, if anybody were going to write music to Kafka's *Metamorphosis,* or based on it, it would not be that open and fresh. I was just trying to make an analogy between the *course* of the story and the music. Say, "One morning Gregor Samsa awoke feeling strange," and that could go with such an opening phrase. You could make that kind of an analogy, as far as the story is concerned, from beginning to end, but it wouldn't have the quality of the story. You're absolutely right.

Q. The second thing: In regard to the closeness of your unconscious and creativity in terms of the performing art—wouldn't it be, kind of disastrous if an interpretative artist, playing a piano concerto, for example, or a violin concerto, were in a trance state like that? Or do you think it would be a necessary condition?

L.B.

Well, I think you've misunderstood me. Because, obviously, the unconscious state—er, no—the semiconscious state in which ideas occur and fructify is not the state in which the piece gets written. You see, if I remained there in that supine position, having gotten the idea, the piece would never get down on paper. Eventually, alas, I have to get up and drag myself over to the desk, take pen and ink and write it down, as Alice in Wonderland said, and go through all the "not inspiration but perspiration" that it takes in order to work an idea into a complete form. But that's something like what an artist does who is performing. He can get ideas or conceptions of the piece in this state, but when he comes to perform, he has to be in control, he has to know what he is doing. If something goes wrong, he has to have enough control so he can correct it immediately. Does that answer your question?

Q. You were talking so much about the trance, or semiconscious state. Would you say, then, that the essence of creativity is passive—

    L.B.

Oh, no.

Q. We didn't hear the question.

    L.B.

The question is: Am I implying by talking so much about a trance that creativity is basically a passive state? Have I quoted you correctly?

Q. Yes.

    L.B.

No. Possibly I wasn't clear. The body may be passive, resting in this supine position, but this is the most extraordinary activity that goes on. How can I describe it to you? It's so mysterious, this creative act. No one has really ever described it well. I think Thomas Mann came pretty close to it in *Dr. Faustus,* but that was under such extraordinary conditions that it doesn't apply to everybody. The creative act, if it's really creative, is something that seizes you, and it is active. It is passive only in the sense that you are somehow a slave of it. In other words, this compulsion causes you to be passive only in the sense that you are in the clutches of something. But I wish I could convey to you the excitement and insane joy of it, which nothing else touches—not making love, not that wonderful glass of orange juice in the morning; nothing! Nothing touches the extraordinary, jubilant sensation of being caught up in this thing—so that you're not just inside yourself, not just lying there. Let's say that you get an idea and you go to the piano and you start with it; and you don't know what you're going to do next, and then you're doing something else next, and you can't stop doing the next thing, and you don't know why. It's madness and it's marvelous. There's nothing in the world like it.

Q. To what extent can you induce this consciously, or is it something—

    L.B.

To no extent. Isn't it awful? And the guy who invents a way of inducing it is going to make a fortune, because this is something that any creative person would give his right arm for. There are ways of inducing it, in one sense—getting back to the Buddhists and the Zen archers—there are certain disciplines that Eastern mystics impose on themselves. There are such things as yoga, and peyote and other drugs; and there are ways in which some people, through meditation, concentration, discipline, and inner control, can get themselves to a point of loss of ego (which I suppose is what it amounts to) by identification with something much further away or closer, depending on how you look at it, something much more inner, so that things will begin to happen. But still there's no guarantee that that's going to turn out F sharps.

Q. Did you ever consciously put emotion into your music?

L.B.

Not consciously—but unconsciously, oh, yes! You see that's a very interesting question you ask. So much has been said and written about letting off steam through art. It sounds like a rather superficial way of explaining the *grande rage,* as the French say, the great rage, which occupies titanic works of art. But one can conceive of Michelangelo making the statue of David in a rage, with zest, beside himself. One can conceive of Beethoven (especially Beethoven, he's the natural one to conceive of being in a rage) and his ferocity in the Fifth Symphony. It's that kind of music. That's rage. That's a man with a tremendous amount of hostility to get off his chest. And he's getting it off—not consciously, not because he's said, "I feel mad today," but in an unconscious way. He is writing, and this sort of thing comes out.

A couple of weeks ago *Time* magazine asked me why I carry on so when I conduct certain kinds of music? It was Beethoven, I think, I was conducting, and it was a piece that contained a lot of rage. And it suddenly occurred to me in discussing it that this probably saved my life as far as unreleased or repressed hostility goes. Because I can do things in the performance of music, and so can any conductor or performer, that if I did on an ordinary street would land me in jail. In other words, I can fume and rage and storm at a hundred men in an orchestra and *mmmmmmm*ake them play this or that chord, and get rid of all kinds of tensions and hostilities. By the time I come to the end of Beethoven's Fifth, I'm a new man. Whereas if I did that down on Seventh Avenue, I'd be picked up.

This is a very lucky kind of profession. You can also do this in composition. But you can't do it, as you say, consciously. There is no way you can say, "Today's my day to be getting rid of hostilities, and between ten and eleven I shall throw my fit, and by eleven-thirty I'll be all right." You either do or you don't.

Q. Can you do justice to music you are conducting when your hostility is expressed, maybe overlapping the music?

L.B.

No, I guess you can't. But, you see, you're making this expression of hostility, or release of hostility, a deliberate force, and it isn't. It happens, as I say, unconsciously, and is part of the general procedure. If by releasing this hostility, you're making *that* the core of the act of conducting, then, of course, you're right. Then there's absolutely no way you can control the music. But I can remember Koussevitzky conducting a Tchaikovsky symphony sometime when he was in his greatest *rage*. He was very fond of that word. That's why I said it in French, I now realize, because Koussevitzky used to use this word. "*En rage,*" he said. "It vas vunderful tonight, Lenuschka, vas it not? I vas in a *rage!*" And I knew what he meant. He came to the piece with something special that he had to let go of. This extra thing was to be gotten rid of, but it was never out of control, and those were the greatest performances. And when the downbeat came, it was as though the earth had split. Nothing less than that. It was so stored up, and the tension had grown, so that the release was an earthquake. Now, that's good only if the composer has asked for a release like an earthquake. There's when you're right. And if you give an earthquake where it is not needed, then you should go back to selling neckties. Yes? Do you mind if I smoke?

Q. Is the trance state something that one could learn to induce in oneself?

L.B.

Well, I thought I answered that before. That would be the ideal situation, if you could do it, but it's not anything you can learn to do. That is something that you hope to arrive at. That would be heaven, if you could do that.

Q. Do you have to lie down to attain creativity?

L.B.

Well, I can tell you, for example, that many of the best musical ideas I have had have not come from lying down at all. As a matter of fact, the opening tune of *Fancy Free,* which is one I like to think of, came to me—just like that—in the Russian Tea Room, when I was having lunch and when I wasn't thinking about anything or lying down anywhere. I think I was in the middle of a conversation about nothing. I wrote it on a napkin, took it home, and wrote the whole first movement. But that doesn't mean that I wasn't in this state. I could have been having a conversation with a certain part of me, but I could have been just enough relaxed so that something could have happened at that moment. It's very hard to describe. You see, sometimes the idea will come at the piano. A composer goes to the keyboard, and nothing occurs to him. The usual thing he will do, if he is a pianist, is that he will sit at the piano and just improvise anything. Many composers use tape recorders and just have them run for about an hour as they do this, improvising for an hour, then playing it back. Perhaps something will sound good, and they pick it out. This is a rather practical way of trying to remember the fantasy, you see. There are many degrees of objectivity and subjectivity that enter into this process, but the main thing is that you be able to be relaxed enough so that you're not looking. So that it all happens while you're not looking. If you're looking, nothing will happen. You see, you try to catch yourself when you think you're not looking. There's something schizoid about the whole thing, and this is why so many composers are loony! . . . Oh, it's very late. One more question.

Q. Do you think it is possible that through the conscious listening to music you could reverse the order of the creative process?

L.B.

And get back to the stage the composer was in when he wrote it, through the music you're hearing? Is that what you're trying to say? I guess it's conceivable. That's a very mystical idea. I think that's more mystical than anything I've said.